Dark Side of Vienna

Unique Walks

Maximilian Just

URBAN
EXPEDITION
EUROPE

Cover and design by JUSTePublishing

Published by JUSTePublishing

Printed in the United States of America

First edition, 2025

CONTENTS

INTRODUCTION TO THE DARK SIDE OF IMPERIAL CITY

But beneath its polished surface, beyond the glitter of Baroque facades and the grace of its music, lies another Vienna—a Vienna most visitors never see. It is a city where shadows stretch long, and the stories they tell are ones of terror, madness, cruelty, and untold secrets. This is the Vienna that doesn't make it into tourist brochures. It is a city haunted by its darker side, where history has not only celebrated triumphs but also borne witness to unspeakable horrors.

Dark Side of Vienna: Unique Walks invites you to step off the well-trodden tourist path and into the hidden heart of this city. This is not the Vienna of postcard-perfect palaces and festive Christmas markets, but of narrow alleyways where dark events unfolded, and forgotten tombstones that still whisper of the tragedies that took place. It is a Vienna where beauty and darkness dance together, casting long, enigmatic shadows that challenge the romanticized image most of us carry.

Our journey begins with the *Habsburg Pharaohs of the Danube*, rulers whose lust for power and control knew no bounds. Their story is one of ambition, but also of tragedy—palaces built on dreams that turned to dust. These rulers, like the pharaohs of ancient Egypt, sought to leave behind legacies of eternal grandeur, but they, too, were human, subject to madness, cruelty, and obsession. Their secrets are woven into the very fabric of Vienna's history, a reminder that even those who ruled from gilded thrones were not immune to darkness.

Schönbrunn Palace and Gardens – a site that played a crucial role in shaping the world as we know it today.

Have you ever considered that both of the wars, the only ones truly worthy of being called world wars (WWI and WWII) due to their immense loss of life and global impact, were initiated by men born in Austria, a small country in the heart of Europe? And did you know that these two men lived in the same city at the same time? That city was Vienna, and the time was right after the First World War. However, during that same period, Vienna was also home to other figures who would go on to be responsible for millions of deaths just a few years later.

We step into a chapter of history where three men—Franz Joseph, Hitler, and Stalin—crossed paths in Vienna, setting into motion a chain of events that would alter the course of human history. This

Fateful Meeting is a chilling reminder of how one city can become the backdrop for world-changing events, where the future of millions is decided in moments.

The gateway to the cemetery of those who chose to pass into eternity in anonymity.

As we wander deeper into Vienna's darker corners, we encounter the *Cemetery of the Nameless*, a forgotten resting place for those whose lives ended tragically in the cold waters of the Danube. These are the souls whose names have been lost to history, but their stories still cry out to be heard. Their cemetery is a silent witness to Vienna's hidden tragedies—a place where the weight of forgotten lives presses down on every visitor who dares to explore.

And then, we arrive at the turmoil of *Vienna in the Great War*, a city transformed by the devastation of global conflict. Once filled with imperial grandeur, Vienna's streets became battlegrounds of survival and despair. The scars of this war can still be felt today in the echoes of the buildings, the faded monuments, and the collective memory of a city that endured immense suffering.

The journey continues as we enter the world of *Sigmund Freud*, whose groundbreaking theories were born in the cafes and salons of Vienna. Freud, perhaps more than anyone, understood that darkness is not only external—it lives within us, too. His exploration of the unconscious mind, repression, and the darker impulses of human behavior forever changed the way we view ourselves and our inner struggles. To walk the streets Freud once wandered is to step into a city where the line between sanity and madness has always been blurred.

But Vienna's shadows are not limited to the distant past. In the *Dark History of Judenplatz*, we confront centuries of persecution, betrayal, and violence against Vienna's Jewish community.

The New Wing of the Hofburg Palace, featuring the balcony from which Hitler gave his infamous speech during the annexation of Austria.

From there, we descend into one of the most horrific periods in Vienna's history: the *Nazi Era*. The atrocities of this time cannot be ignored, and their legacy casts a long, dark shadow over the city. The reminders of these horrors are scattered throughout Vienna, a city that was once a battleground for hatred and survival.

Yet, Vienna's dark history stretches back even further. The *Two Sieges by the Ottoman Army* nearly brought the city to its knees, as it teetered on the edge of annihilation. These battles left an indelible mark on the city's psyche, as it fought to preserve itself against overwhelming odds.

Belvedere – the palace of Prince Eugene of Savoy, the man who put an end to Ottoman expansion on the European continent once and for all.

In contrast to these epic struggles, we encounter a more intimate terror: *Elisabeth Báthory, The Blood Countess*. Her story is one of unimaginable cruelty, a tale that continues to fascinate and horrify in equal measure. Báthory's acts of sadism left a bloody stain on history, reminding us that even in the elegant courts of Europe, darkness was never far away.

From the blood-soaked legends of aristocracy, we turn to the cold logic of crime at *Vienna's Kriminalmuseum*, where the most gruesome and unsettling stories of the city's criminals are preserved. The chilling details of Vienna's dark underbelly are laid bare in this museum, a place where justice and cruelty collide.

No journey into the heart of Vienna's shadows would be complete without a visit to the *Funeral Museum*, where the Viennese obsession with death takes center stage. The city's intricate funeral customs, bizarre burial practices, and deep-rooted fascination with mortality are unlike anything else in the world. In Vienna, death is not just an end—it is a spectacle, a ritual to be honored and remembered.

And finally, we reach the *Zentralfriedhof*, Vienna's city of the dead, where the deceased far outnumber the living. Among the grand tombs of Beethoven and Johann Strauss lie the forgotten, the disgraced, and the tragic. Walking through this vast cemetery is like walking through the soul of Vienna itself, a city haunted by its past, yet unable to let go.

The graves of Beethoven, Mozart, and Franz Schubert.

Vienna is a city that never forgets its dead, and its dark history continues to shape its present. To truly understand this city, you must confront not only its beauty but also its shadows. *Dark Side of Vienna: Unique Walks* invites you to take that step—to uncover the hidden stories, the forgotten tragedies, and the darker truths that lurk beneath the surface.

Are you ready to explore Vienna, which history books often overlook? Are you curious enough to journey into the shadows of a city where every beautiful façade hides a darker story?

Grab your guide today and take your first step into Vienna's hidden world—a world where beauty and darkness waltz together in an eternal dance.

DEATH AS A COMPANION: LIFE OF FRANZ JOSEPH

Franz Joseph I (1830–1916) was Emperor of Austria, King of Hungary, and ruler of the other states of the Habsburg monarchy. His reign, from 1848 to 1916, spanned nearly seven decades. Over such a long period, countless events can shape a ruler's life, yet the personal tragedies Franz Joseph endured are exceptional, even by royal standards.

The emperor's first violent encounter with death occurred when he was just 22 years old. On February 18, 1853, Franz Joseph was walking outside Vienna's city walls with his adjutant, Count O'Donnell, when an assassination attempt unfolded.

A Hungarian tailor's apprentice, János Libényi, attacked the emperor with a kitchen knife, aiming for his neck. However, the stiff, high collar of Franz Joseph's uniform—a feature of contemporary fashion—saved his life, allowing the knife to only graze the skin. Count O'Donnell, assisted by a passerby, quickly subdued the attacker. Libényi was charged with attempted regicide and executed by hanging on February 26, 1853.

The execution site, known as "Spinnerin am Kreuz," remains a historical marker on Vienna's Triesterstraße.

Emperor Franz Joseph (1851)

Aftermath

For his bravery, Count O'Donnell, previously an Irish noble, was granted an Austrian title. Similarly, Josef Ettenreich, the butcher who helped overpower Libényi, was ennobled for his actions. The failed assassination even inspired Johann Strauss II to compose the *Kaiser Franz Joseph I. Rettungs-Jubelmarsch* (Op. 126), which incorporated the Austrian imperial anthem.

Franz Joseph's younger brother, Maximilian, took the initiative to commemorate the event by organizing a fundraising campaign for the construction of a grand church at the site of the attack. This effort sparked widespread patriotic enthusiasm across the empire, and the necessary funds were quickly collected. The resulting Votive Church (*Votivkirche*), completed in 1879, stands at Vienna's Schottentor and is one of the city's most impressive landmarks, surpassing many European cathedrals in scale and grandeur.

This episode is just one of many tragic and peculiar events that shaped the emperor's life. The story continues with Franz Joseph's brother Maximilian, whose own fate became one of the most bizarre chapters in the history of the Habsburg dynasty.

Maximilian von Habsburg-Lothringen: The Brother (1867)

Maximilian, the younger brother of Emperor Franz Joseph, seemed destined never to live a peaceful life. His tumultuous existence began even before his birth, spanned his entire life, and left echoes long after his death. Maximilian was, in many ways, the wrong man in the wrong place—a tragic figure trapped in a life resembling a dark Mexican soap opera.

Maximilian spent much of his life in the shadow of his elder brother Franz Joseph. Like many second-born royals, he struggled with frustration and a sense of unfulfilled purpose. To escape his brother's shadow, Maximilian retreated to the port city of Trieste, far from Vienna and the imperial court that would never truly belong to him. There, he sought distance and purpose, but fate had other plans.

Naval Aspirations and Early Losses: Maximilian served as commander-in-chief of the Imperial Austrian Navy and was briefly the Austrian viceroy of Lombardy-Venetia. However, his tenure as viceroy was cut short by his brother, Franz Joseph, who removed him from the position. Maximilian's life was not only marked by political disappointments but also deeply personal losses.

In Lisbon, Maximilian fell in love with Princess Maria Amélia of Braganza, the daughter of Brazil's Emperor Pedro I. Franz Joseph and their domineering mother, Archduchess Sophie, approved of the potential marriage. Tragically, Maria Amélia contracted scarlet fever which later developed into tuberculosis. She passed away and Maximilian was heartbroken.

This loss shaped his outlook and drove him further from Vienna. He spent significant time in Paris, where he mingled with European elites and sought solace. However, his family had other plans, and Franz Joseph summoned him back to Vienna—via Brussels, where Maximilian met Princess Charlotte of Belgium. This union was politically favorable, and the two were soon married.

A Throne in a Foreign Land: Maximilian's path to Mexico began with a meeting in Paris with French Emperor Napoleon III. Mexican conservatives, eager to restore a monarchy, sought a European royal to lead their nation and approached Napoleon for a candidate. History books often repeat the justification for Maximilian's candidacy, emphasizing his lineage as a descendant of Charles V, Holy Roman Emperor and Spanish King. Charles V had ruled Mexico as part of the Spanish Empire during its conquest of the Aztec Empire in the early 16th century. This tenuous connection was used to frame Maximilian as a suitable ruler. Maximilian agreed to the plan but only on the condition of guaranteed French support.

Archduchess Sophie of Bavaria (1832)

Why did Napoleon III specifically choose Maximilian to be entangled in the Mexican turmoil? It seemed there was a particular reason behind his decision. At the Viennese court, they were well aware of the true motives.

Rumors of Parentage: Maximilian's life was further complicated by rumors surrounding his origins. His mother, Archduchess Sophie of Bavaria, was known for her strong-willed nature and iron grip on the Habsburg court. Rumors abounded that she had an affair with Franz, Duke of Reichstadt—better known as Napoleon II, the son of Napoleon Bonaparte. The striking physical resemblance between Maximilian and Napoleon II only fueled speculation. Just days after Maximilian's birth, Napoleon II died, allegedly of tuberculosis, at the age of 21.

A Doomed Reign: After being persuaded by Napoleon III, Maximilian and Charlotte set sail for Mexico, where he was proclaimed Emperor Maximilian I in 1864. His reign was brief and turbulent. Mexico was deeply divided, with republicans under Benito Juárez opposing the monarchy. Despite French military support initially backing Maximilian, the situation quickly deteriorated as French troops withdrew under pressure from the United States.

Abandoned and isolated, Maximilian refused to abdicate, believing his rule was divinely sanctioned. Captured by republican forces in 1867, he faced a court-martial and was sentenced to death. On June 19, 1867, Maximilian was executed by firing squad in Querétaro, Mexico.

Aftermath

Maximilian's wife, Charlotte of Belgium, Empress of Mexico, was in Europe at the time of his death. She was attempting to gain support for her husband and their empire through personal meetings with Emperor Napoleon III of France and the Pope in the Vatican. Both refused to meet with her, and she was placed under house arrest at her castle, Miramare, in Trieste. Declared mentally unstable and psychologically ill, she was later moved to Belgium, where she spent the rest of her life in a psychiatric institution until her death in 1927. Rumors persist that she was unjustly declared insane but ultimately succumbed to mental instability after years of isolation.

Before his death in 1867, Maximilian reportedly had an affair with a Mexican woman, who bore him a son. The boy was secretly taken to France by Mexican royalists, where he was raised. However, inheriting the misfortune of his father and grandfather, his life ended in a similarly tragic manner. During World War I, while living in Spain, he was recruited by German intelligence. Arrested by the French as a traitor, he was executed by firing squad in 1917. According to an account by a biographer, though without cited sources, the charge read at his execution began, "Sedano, son of Emperor Maximilian of Mexico."

Following Maximilian's execution, Austrian Admiral Wilhelm von Tegetthoff was dispatched to Mexico aboard the SMS *Novara* to retrieve the emperor's body. After arriving in Trieste, the coffin was transported to Vienna and placed in the Imperial Crypt.

Lisbon's Rossio Square

A monument to Maximilian stands in Lisbon's main square, though its creation, like much of his life, is steeped in peculiar circumstances. Maximilian's would-be father-in-law, the father of the love of his life who died shortly after meeting him, was Pedro I, the first emperor of Brazil. Born in Lisbon, Pedro was also recognized for a time as King Pedro IV of Portugal. In honor of this "illustrious son of the nation," it was decided to erect a monument in Lisbon in the style of Trajan's Column in the city's central square. Atop the column, a statue of King Pedro IV was to be placed.

A renowned French sculptor, famous for crafting unforgettable statues of heroes, was commissioned for the task. Allegedly, the sculptor had already completed a statue of Maximilian of Mexico, which had no recipient due to his untimely death. With minor modifications, he presented the statue as Pedro IV to Portugal. This story, as the saying goes, is an urban legend. For skeptics of the official narrative, it is said that if you bring binoculars to Lisbon's Rossio Square, you might glimpse the face of Maximilian atop the column instead of Pedro IV.

Rudolf von Habsburg: The Son (1889)

Rudolf, Crown Prince of Austria (1858–1889), was the heir to the Habsburg throne and the only son of Emperor Franz Joseph and Empress Elisabeth. When he turned 30, tragedy struck.

In 1886, Rudolf purchased Mayerling, a hunting lodge. By late 1888, the 30-year-old Crown Prince had begun an affair with

17-year-old Baroness Marie von Vetsera. On January 30, 1889, their bodies were discovered at the lodge, apparently the result of a joint suicide. To avoid the stigma of suicide and the denial of a church burial, Rudolf was officially declared to have been in a state of "mental unbalance" and was interred in the Imperial Crypt in Vienna.

Rudolf of Austria (1887)

Vetsera's body was secretly removed from Mayerling during the night and buried in the village cemetery of Heiligenkreuz. Following the tragedy, Emperor Franz Joseph had Mayerling transformed into a Carmelite convent, with an endowed chantry to ensure daily prayers by the nuns for the repose of Rudolf's soul.

Rudolf's valet, Johann Loschek, later recounted: *"Throughout the night, I heard Rudolf and Vetsera speaking in very serious tones. I couldn't make out the words. Five minutes before a quarter to seven in the morning, Rudolf came to my room, fully dressed, and ordered the carriage to be prepared. I hadn't yet stepped into the courtyard when I heard two gunshots. I ran back immediately, smelling gunpowder as I approached. I stormed toward the bedroom, but, unusually, the door was locked."*

Rudolf had long used morphine and cocaine suppositories, as well as opium-based gargles, and was known for heavy drinking. He suffered from severe mood swings, his marriage was in ruins, and his conservative father excluded him from state affairs, despite Rudolf's keen interest in politics and liberal ideas.

Aftermath

In 2015, Vetsera's private letters were discovered in a safe deposit box at an Austrian bank. These letters confirmed her intent to commit suicide with Rudolf out of love, providing clarity on her role in the tragic events at Mayerling.

Speculation about a political conspiracy has persisted over the years, fueled in part by the Habsburg family itself. Zita, the last Habsburg Empress, accused French Prime Minister Georges Clemenceau of orchestrating the murder, alleging Rudolf refused to participate in a plot against his father, Emperor Franz Joseph.

However, the frequent signs of psychological instability in the Habsburg family could not be entirely dismissed. These issues were often attributed to the centuries of intermarriage practiced to preserve wealth and power within the dynasty. The medical term "Habsburg jaw" is a well-documented example of the physical consequences of inbreeding among close relatives.

With this tragedy, we move on to the next somber chapter in the life of Franz Joseph.

Empress Elisabeth-Sisi: The Wife (1898)

The most beautiful woman of the 19th century, as her contemporaries called her, was born as Duchess Elisabeth Amalie Eugenie in Bavaria. It is no coincidence that her title was almost identical to that of her husband's mother—Elisabeth's mother and Franz Joseph's mother were sisters.

Thus, the Habsburg tradition of cousins marrying cousins continued, as tradition was of utmost importance in ruling families. Franz Joseph and Elisabeth lived more apart than together, likely contributing to a harmonious marriage that lasted 44 years. And then, tragedy struck.

Empress Elisabeth-Sisi (1865)

The Empress traveled incognito to Geneva. Her visit did not escape the notice of the hotel staff, some of whom indiscreetly tipped off the local newspapers.

At the same time, an Italian anarchist named Luigi Lucheni was in Geneva, determined to make a name for himself. He gave the following statement to the police:

"I am an anarchist by conviction... I came to Geneva to kill a sovereign, with the object of giving an example to those who suffer and those who do nothing to improve their social position; it did not matter to me who the sovereign was whom I should kill... It was not a woman I struck, but an Empress; it was a crown that I had in view."

Lucheni had initially planned to assassinate the Duke of Orléans, the pretender to the French throne, but the duke had left Geneva for Valais. Unable to find his original target, Lucheni turned his attention to Elisabeth after a Geneva newspaper revealed that the elegant woman traveling under the pseudonym "Countess of Hohenembs" was the Empress of Austria.

Elisabeth and her lady-in-waiting left their hotel on the shores of Lake Geneva on foot to catch the steamship *Genève* bound for Montreux. As Elisabeth disliked processions, she insisted on walking without the rest of her entourage.

While walking along the promenade, Lucheni approached the pair, pretending to stumble as he attempted to peer under Elisabeth's parasol. As the ship's bell signaled its departure, Lucheni feigned losing his balance and thrust a sharpened needle file into Elisabeth's heart.

When Franz Joseph received the telegram informing him of Elisabeth's death, his first fear was that she had committed suicide. Only after a second message detailed the assassination was he reassured on that point. The telegram also requested permission to perform an autopsy, to which Franz Joseph replied that all prescribed procedures should be followed.

Aftermath

Empress Elisabeth was laid to rest in the Imperial Crypt in Vienna, her tomb placed beside that of her husband, Franz Joseph. On her other side lies their son, Crown Prince Rudolf.

Mark Twain, who witnessed Elisabeth's funeral procession from the balcony of his room at the Hotel Ambassador (still located opposite the Imperial Crypt), described her as:

"So beautiful, in mind and heart, in person and spirit; and whether with a crown upon her head or without it and nameless, a grace to the human race."

The Question of Succession: The Brothers

After Crown Prince Rudolf's death in 1889, Emperor Franz Joseph lacked a direct heir, forcing the succession to pass to his brothers. His brother Maximilian had been executed in Mexico in 1867, and his second brother, Ludwig, was unsuitable due to his lifestyle, which caused persistent gossip in Vienna.

The breaking point came when a public altercation at Vienna's Central Bath led to Ludwig's exile to Salzburg, ending his role at court. Franz Joseph then named his third brother, Karl Ludwig, as heir. However, Karl Ludwig died in 1896 after contracting a fatal infection from contaminated Jordan River water during a pilgrimage.

Franz Ferdinand: The Nephew (1914)

After the death of Emperor Franz Joseph's brother, Karl Ludwig, his nephew Franz Ferdinand was declared the new heir to the throne. However, Franz Ferdinand did little to endear himself to his uncle, the Emperor.

Franz Ferdinand (1914)

Franz Ferdinand had two main hobbies. He was passionate about driving cars at the highest possible speeds and had an obsession with hunting.

His enthusiasm for trophy hunting was excessive, even by the standards of European nobility. He meticulously recorded his kills in his diaries, boasting a staggering total of 272,511, including 5,000 deer. Around 100,000 hunting trophies were displayed at his castle in Bohemia, serving as a testament to his relentless pursuit of game.

Adding to the tensions with his uncle, Franz Ferdinand chose a wife who did not meet the strict expectations of the imperial family.

To marry into the House of Habsburg, one had to belong to a reigning or formerly reigning European dynasty. Sophie Chotek's family, the Choteks, did not qualify. Nevertheless, Franz Ferdinand, deeply in love, refused to consider any other match. His courtship of Sophie caused significant conflict within the imperial household. Their morganatic marriage in 1900 was permitted only after Franz Ferdinand renounced his descendants' rights to the throne.

The Assassination: On Sunday, June 28, 1914, Franz Ferdinand and Sophie were assassinated in Sarajevo, the capital of the Austro-Hungarian province of Bosnia and Herzegovina. The assassin,

Gavrilo Princip, was a member of the revolutionary group Young Bosnia, which had been trained and armed by a secret Serbian officers' organization known as the Black Hand.

Emperor Franz Joseph (1892)

Aftermath

The assassination of the heir to the throne was an act the empire could not forgive. Emperor Franz Joseph issued the proclamation *To My Peoples*, declaring war on Serbia. This marked the beginning of World War I, a conflict that not only engulfed his empire but also drew three other empires into the bloodiest war humanity had seen up to that time.

Franz Joseph's personal tragedies likely influenced his decision to take such drastic action. He died in 1916, before the war's end, and was buried in the Imperial Crypt, alongside nearly all his Habsburg relatives.

THE HABSBURG PHARAOHS OF THE DANUBE

The Habsburg tradition of dividing their remains across three sacred sites—bodies in the Imperial Crypt, hearts in the Augustinian Church, and viscera in St. Stephen's Cathedral—has drawn comparisons to the burial practices of ancient Egyptian pharaohs. Like the pharaohs, the Habsburgs sought to maintain their power and influence beyond death by ensuring that their physical remains were enshrined in the most important religious sites of their empire.

This division of body, heart, and viscera reflects not only the religious beliefs of the time but also the Habsburgs' desire to leave a lasting legacy. By entombing themselves in multiple locations, they ensured that their presence would remain felt across Vienna, long after the fall of their empire. Today, these burial sites stand as poignant reminders of the dynasty's once-great power and its deep connection to the city of Vienna. The Habsburgs may no longer rule, but their remains—spread across these sacred spaces—continue to tell the story of their enduring influence over European history.

Schönbrunn Palace was commissioned by Maria Theresa as a summer residence for her large family.

Throughout European history, the Habsburg dynasty remains one of the most powerful and influential royal families. For centuries, they ruled vast territories, including the Austro-Hungarian Empire, and left an indelible mark on politics, art, architecture, and culture. While much has been written about their reign and contributions to European history, one of the more intriguing aspects of the Habsburg legacy is their unique burial tradition.

This tradition, similar in some ways to the elaborate burial customs of the Egyptian pharaohs, involved dividing their bodies into three separate locations: the body, heart, and viscera were interred in different sacred sites. This custom, rooted in both religious and dynastic symbolism, created a profound link between the Habsburgs and some of Vienna's most significant historical landmarks.

Among the most important of these burial sites are the Augustinian Church (Augustinerkirche), St. Stephen's Cathedral (Stephansdom), and the Imperial Crypt (Kapuzinergruft). Together, these locations form a triad that tells the story of how the Habsburgs viewed death, the afterlife, and their enduring presence within the heart of their empire.

The Augustinian Church: Hearts of the Habsburgs

The Augustinian Church, located in Vienna's Hofburg Palace complex, was not only a significant religious center for the Habsburgs during their lifetimes but also in their deaths. While this Gothic church is most famously known for its role in Habsburg weddings and religious ceremonies, it is also home to the *Herzgruft* (Heart Crypt), where the hearts of 54 members of the Habsburg family are kept in silver urns. This practice of preserving and entombing the heart separately from the body symbolizes the intimate connection between the Habsburg rulers and the people they governed.

In the Augustinian Church, the former court parish church, you'll also find the memorial to Archduchess Maria Christina of Austria, created by Antonio Canova in 1805.

The church itself played host to some of the most important milestones in the lives of the Habsburgs. Empress Maria Theresa married Francis Stephan of Lorraine here, as did Emperor Franz Joseph I and Empress Elisabeth (Sisi). Crown Prince Rudolf, Franz Joseph's ill-fated son, married Princess Stephanie in the Augustinian Church, and even the French Emperor Napoleon Bonaparte was married to his Habsburgian wife, Marie-Louise, within its walls. These weddings symbolized the dynastic power of the Habsburgs and their influence across Europe.

Yet, it is the presence of the Heart Crypt that adds a deeper layer of significance. The tradition of removing and separately preserving the heart goes back to medieval times, rooted in the idea that the heart, as the seat of emotions and spirit, deserved a place of special reverence. In the Augustinian Church, the hearts of the Habsburgs remain, metaphorically binding the family to the city and its people long after their earthly power has faded.

In 2004, the church's historical connection to the Habsburgs was further honored with the dedication of a new side altar to Blessed Emperor Charles I, the last emperor of Austria. The Habsburg legacy thus continues, with the church playing an essential role in preserving both the spiritual and historical heritage of the dynasty.

The Imperial Crypt: Bodies of the Habsburgs

The Imperial Crypt, also known as the Kapuzinergruft, lies beneath the Capuchin Church (Kapuzinerkirche) and serves as the primary burial site for Habsburg monarchs and their closest family members. Since 1633, the crypt has housed the remains of 12 emperors, 19 empresses, and numerous other members of the Habsburg dynasty. This sacred space is not only a place of burial but also a gallery of Habsburg power and influence, with tombs reflecting the distinct artistic styles of the Baroque, Rococo, and Neoclassical periods.

One of the most fascinating aspects of Habsburg burials is the unique "admission ceremony" that takes place upon the death of a royal family member. When the body of a Habsburg arrives at the crypt, a Capuchin friar stands behind the closed doors and asks, "Who seeks admittance?" A herald then lists the deceased's full title, which is rejected with the reply, "We do not know of them." Only when the herald humbly responds, "A poor sinner," is the door opened, symbolizing the rejection of worldly power in the face of death and divine judgment.

The Imperial Crypt

The crypt itself is a stunning juxtaposition of imperial grandeur and macabre humility. Empress Maria Theresa's tomb, for example, is a grand baroque masterpiece, reflecting her political and cultural achievements, while the tomb of her son, Emperor Joseph II, is stark and simple, befitting his Enlightenment ideals. The crypt also contains the remains of the last emperor, Franz Joseph I, who is buried alongside his beloved wife, Empress Elisabeth, and their tragic son, Crown Prince Rudolf.

This tradition of burying the body separately from the heart and viscera underscores the Habsburgs' complex relationship with death and the afterlife.

The sarcophagus of Empress Maria Theresa.

It allowed them to be physically present in multiple sacred locations across Vienna, thus maintaining a lasting connection to the people, the church, and the dynasty.

St. Stephen's Cathedral: The Viscera of the Habsburgs

While the bodies and hearts of the Habsburgs found their final resting places in the Imperial Crypt and the Augustinian Church, the viscera—the internal organs—were entombed in St. Stephen's Cathedral, Vienna's most iconic religious structure.

The practice of separating the viscera from the body was not unique to the Habsburgs but was a common European practice for royalty and nobility in the medieval and early modern periods.

The catacombs beneath St. Stephen's Cathedral house the urns containing the viscera of Habsburg rulers from 1564 to 1878. This practice of dividing the remains into three parts symbolized the dispersal of the royal person into the physical, spiritual, and visceral realms.

The entrance to the catacombs of St. Stephen's Cathedral (Stephansdom)

St. Stephen's Cathedral, with its towering Gothic spires and historical significance, was the natural place to hold such a sacred relic.

St. Stephen's Cathedral has always been a central part of Habsburg life and death. It was here that many Habsburgs were baptized, married, and mourned. The cathedral's grandiose architecture and deep connection to the Habsburg legacy made it a fitting resting place for the visceral remains of the dynasty.

Walking tour

1. Stephansdom | St. Stephen's Cathedral

Historical Significance: St. Stephen's Cathedral is Vienna's most famous Gothic landmark. Its catacombs serve as the resting place for the internal organs of members of the Habsburg dynasty, in accordance with royal burial customs.

Address: Stephansplatz 3, 1010 Vienna

Public transport: U1, U3 to Stephansplatz

Opening hours: Mon-Sat: 6 a.m. – 10 p.m.; Sun: 7 a.m. – 10 p.m.

Online: www.stephansdom.at

Next Stop: Kapuzinergruft | Imperial Crypt

Distance: 650 m (0.4 miles)

Walking Time: ~8 minutes

2. Kapuzinergruft | Imperial Crypt

Historical Significance: The Kapuzinergruft, or Imperial Crypt, is the final resting place of the Habsburg emperors and empresses. This crypt contains the bodies of many Habsburg family members, including Empress Maria Theresa and Emperor Franz Joseph I.

Address: Tegetthoffstraße 2, 1010 Vienna
Public transport: U1, U3 to Stephansplatz
Opening hours: Mon-Sun: 10 a.m. – 6 p.m.
Online: www.kaisergruft.at
Next Stop: Augustinerkirche | Augustinian Church
Distance: 350 m (0.22 miles)
Walking Time: ~5 minutes

3. Augustinerkirche | Augustinian Church

Historical Significance: Augustinerkirche was the royal wedding church of the Habsburgs. It also houses the Herzgruft, or Heart Crypt, where the hearts of 54 Habsburg family members are preserved. The church played an essential role in Habsburg religious life and royal ceremonies.

Address: Augustinerstraße 3, 1010 Vienna
Public transport: U1, U3 to Stephansplatz
Opening hours: Daily: 7 a.m. – 7 p.m.
Online: www.augustinerkirche.at

A Fateful Meeting: Franz Joseph, Hitler, and Stalin

In the winter of 1913, three of the most influential figures of the 20th century—Emperor Franz Joseph I, Adolf Hitler, and Joseph Stalin—crossed paths in Vienna without recognizing each other. It was a chance meeting that history might have called a cosmic coincidence if its eventual outcomes had not been so tragic. This fascinating intersection of lives occurred in February, in the peaceful Schönbrunn Palace Park. But at the time, no one could have known the seismic shifts in history that would soon be triggered by these three men.

A City of Contrasts

At the dawn of the 20th century, Vienna was the Babylon of the Habsburg Empire—a bustling metropolis of over two million people, known for its cultural brilliance, artistic innovation, and political complexity. It was a vibrant hub of ideas, where nationalists, revolutionaries, artists, and thinkers gathered, shaping the city into a kaleidoscope of activity. Yet, beneath this glittering surface of architectural beauty, operatic masterpieces, and intellectual thought, Vienna was also a city rife with tensions and contradictions.

The capital of the Austro-Hungarian Empire had become a meeting point for a wide array of political ideologies. It was a crossroads for the tensions of its multi-ethnic population—Germans, Hungarians, Slavs, Jews, and other nationalities—vying for their place within a crumbling empire. Franz Joseph I, the monarch of this vast realm, sat on the throne of an empire that appeared to be slipping through his fingers. Vienna, once a seat of power, was on the brink of seeing history's greatest upheavals unfold.

Franz Joseph I: The Dying Monarch

Every morning in 1913, Emperor Franz Joseph I, already an aging symbol of a bygone era, traveled from Schönbrunn Palace to Hofburg Palace, continuing his imperial duties.

Empress Elisabeth (Sisi) on the facade of St. Stephen's Cathedral.

At the age of 83, he had been ruling Austria for 65 years, having ascended the throne in the aftermath of the 1848 revolutions. By 1913, Franz Joseph was a figure steeped in tradition, the embodiment of the Habsburg monarchy's seemingly eternal grasp on power.

However, cracks had begun to show. His reign was marked by personal tragedy—the suicide of his only son, Crown Prince Rudolf, in 1889, and the assassination of his beloved wife, Empress Elisabeth (Sisi), in 1898. These losses weighed heavily on the old emperor, who increasingly retreated to the quiet gardens of Schönbrunn.

Schönbrunn Garden in Winter.

In the winter of 1913, as he rode in his dark green carriage, the emperor would pass through Schönbrunner Schloßstraße, unaware of the events brewing around him. He could not have known that his empire's days were numbered, nor that a mere year later, the assassination of his nephew and heir, Archduke Franz Ferdinand, would lead him to declare war on Serbia—a decision that would plunge Europe into the abyss of World War I.

This decision ultimately set the stage for over 17 million deaths, and marked the beginning of the end for the Habsburg dynasty.

Adolf Hitler: The Failed Artist

During this same winter of 1913, a young Adolf Hitler was also walking through Schönbrunn Park. He was a failed art student, having twice been rejected by the prestigious Vienna Academy of Fine Arts, and was living in a men's home, scraping by on what little money he earned from selling his sketches of Vienna's iconic landmarks.

Hitler's time in Vienna was one of disillusionment. His dreams of becoming a celebrated artist had been crushed, and he was beginning to develop the radical views that would later define his ideology. Spending his days wandering through the streets and parks of Vienna, including the grand Schönbrunn gardens, he nurtured his growing bitterness toward the city's Jewish population, its cosmopolitan elite, and the multi-ethnic makeup of the Austro-Hungarian Empire.

Hitler's close friend from this period, August Kubizek, later recalled how the two of them would watch Franz Joseph ride past in his carriage, never suspecting the profound political impact Hitler would have in the years to come.

By May 1913, Hitler would leave Vienna for Germany, where his rise from a homeless drifter to the leader of the Third Reich would be swift and brutal. Within a few decades, his actions would lead to the outbreak of World War II and the deaths of over 70 million people.

Joseph Stalin: The Revolutionary in Exile

Meanwhile, not far from Schönbrunn, Joseph Stalin—then going by his real name, Joseph Vissarionovich—was living at Schönbrunner Schloßstraße 30. Stalin, a young revolutionary at the time, had already made a name for himself as a bank robber, murderer, and activist for the Bolshevik cause. He had come to Vienna as part of his exile from Russia, and was using the city as a temporary base of operations. It was during this stay in Vienna that Stalin first signed a letter with his new revolutionary pseudonym—Stalin, meaning "man of steel."

Schönbrunner Schloßstraße 30

Every morning, Stalin would stroll through Schönbrunn Park with the daughter of his Viennese host, oblivious to the significance of his surroundings. Stalin was yet to take the reins of power, but in just a few years, his brutal rule would lead to the deaths of over 20 million

Soviet citizens. His tyrannical reign would reshape the Soviet Union, and leave an indelible mark on world history.

The Secret Crossroads of History

In February 1913, these three men—Franz Joseph I, Adolf Hitler, and Joseph Stalin—were in close proximity, each navigating the same streets and paths of Schönbrunn Park. They crossed each other's lives unknowingly, each pursuing their personal destinies that would soon intertwine with the future of Europe and the world.

The significance of this fleeting moment is almost surreal. In the quiet winter mornings of Schönbrunn, the three leaders whose actions would shape the course of the 20th century—bringing about two world wars, the deaths of millions, and the redrawing of Europe's political map—were all walking the same paths. It's as though Vienna, with its rich history and imperial grandeur, provided the backdrop for an apocalyptic convergence.

Café Central

Vienna as a Cauldron of Revolution and Conspiracy

At the time, Vienna was also home to other revolutionary figures. Leon Trotsky, a key figure in the Russian Revolution and the founder of the Red Army, lived in the city from 1906 to 1914. He frequented Café Central, a meeting place for intellectuals and revolutionaries.

Legend has it that in 1917, a Viennese diplomat jokingly remarked, “Who is supposed to start a revolution in Russia? Perhaps that fellow Bronstein from Café Central?”—Bronstein being Trotsky’s real name. Little did the diplomat know that Trotsky would soon help orchestrate one of the most important revolutions in history.

The Great Unnoticed Meeting

As you wander through Schönbrunn Palace Park today, it’s impossible not to wonder what it must have been like in that winter of 1913. Could anyone have imagined that in those tranquil, baroque gardens, the lives of three of the 20th century’s most notorious leaders would briefly intersect? Could anyone have foreseen the devastation that would soon follow?

This chance meeting of Franz Joseph, Hitler, and Stalin in Vienna serves as a haunting reminder of how history often unfolds in unexpected and unseen ways. The fates of nations can pivot on the quietest moments, and the paths of individuals can cross without anyone realizing the seismic shifts that will soon follow.

In that winter of 1913, Vienna played host to not just an imperial ruler, a failed artist, and a revolutionary—but to the future of Europe, and indeed the world.

THE NARRENTURM

The Narrenturm was built in 1784, commissioned by Emperor Joseph II of Austria, a ruler famed for his reforms in education, health care, and governance. As part of his Enlightenment ideals, Joseph II sought to improve medical care throughout his empire. Among his initiatives was the creation of the Allgemeines Krankenhaus (General Hospital) in Vienna, of which the Narrenturm was a part.

Located in Vienna's 9th district, the Narrenturm was constructed as Europe's first psychiatric hospital, and perhaps one of the earliest examples of an institution built specifically for the care of the mentally ill. The term "Narrenturm" itself translates to "Fools' Tower," reflecting the prevailing attitudes toward mental illness at the time. Mental health was poorly understood, and those suffering from it were often shunned, imprisoned, or confined in inhumane conditions. Joseph II's construction of the Narrenturm, while still far from our modern understanding of mental health care, represented a more organized, albeit still primitive, approach to treating mental illness.

Architecturally, the building is unique. The Narrenturm is a circular, five-story tower with 28 cells on each floor. The building's round shape may have been intended to facilitate observation of patients from a central point, which would allow for easier surveillance and control. Patients were housed in cells, often locked in and isolated from one another, reflecting the belief at the time that mental illnesses were dangerous and needed to be physically restrained. Chains and bars were commonly used to keep patients confined within their cells. This environment, though grim by modern standards, was an early attempt to provide a space exclusively for the treatment of mental illness rather than simply imprisoning individuals alongside common criminals.

Early Psychiatric Practices

The methods used to treat patients at the Narrenturm were rudimentary and often brutal. The late 18th and early 19th centuries were times of experimentation in medicine, particularly in the field of psychiatry. There were no scientific understandings of mental illnesses as we know them today. Instead, early psychiatry was based on a combination of superstition, trial and error, and outdated theories of humoral imbalances or demonic possession.

Treatments at the Narrenturm included bloodletting, purging, and physical restraints. The use of chains and straightjackets was common, and patients were often subjected to isolation in small, dark cells. Cold baths and the application of ice were thought to "shock" the brain and restore mental equilibrium. Other techniques involved forced vomiting, blistering, and the use of laxatives to "cleanse" the body of its imbalances. Music therapy and occasional fresh air were also experimented with as potential calming measures.

At the time, mental illness was still largely viewed through the lens of fear and misunderstanding. Many believed that those suffering from conditions like schizophrenia, bipolar disorder, or epilepsy were possessed by evil spirits, and the methods of treatment often reflected attempts to purge these supposed demons. Others subscribed to early neurological theories that saw the brain as an organ requiring "rebalancing" through physical interventions.

The Evolution of Psychiatric Treatment

As the 19th century progressed, so did attitudes toward mental health care, although change came slowly. The late 1800s and early 1900s saw the development of more humane approaches, influenced by figures such as Jean-Martin Charcot and Sigmund Freud, both of whom had strong ties to Vienna's medical community. The concept of "moral treatment," which promoted kindness and respect in the treatment of patients, began to take hold in psychiatric hospitals across Europe. Institutions like the Narrenturm, however, continued to house patients in less-than-ideal conditions until well into the 20th century.

The Narrenturm ceased to function as a psychiatric hospital in the 19th century as newer, more modern psychiatric institutions were built in Vienna.

Today, the Narrenturm serves a different purpose: it is home to the Pathological-Anatomical Museum, a branch of the Natural History Museum of Vienna. The museum's collection includes a wide range of medical oddities, preserved human organs, and anatomical specimens. These exhibits offer insight into the development of medical science, pathology, and anatomy over the centuries.

Visitors to the Narrenturm can view collections of skulls, malformed body parts, and models of diseases that were once common in the population. There are also exhibits on the history of psychiatric treatment, showing the instruments and tools used in early mental health care. The museum serves as a fascinating, if sometimes unsettling, testament to the history of medicine, from its early, rudimentary beginnings to the complex field it is today.

The building itself, with its thick walls, barred windows, and cold stone interiors, remains largely unchanged from its time as a psychiatric hospital. Walking through the tower, it is easy to imagine the lives of the patients who were once housed here, many of whom were locked away in isolation, misunderstood and often mistreated.

Narrenturm | Fool's Tower

Historical Significance: The Narrenturm, built in 1784, is Europe's oldest purpose-built psychiatric hospital. This round tower, commissioned by Emperor Joseph II, reflects Enlightenment-era medical advancements and attitudes toward mental health. Today, it houses the Pathological-Anatomical Museum, showcasing a fascinating and macabre collection of medical artifacts.

Address: Spitalgasse 2, 1090 Vienna

Public transport: U6 to Alser Straße, Tram 43 or 44 to Lange Gasse

Opening hours: Wed-Sun: 10 a.m. – 6 p.m.

Online: https://www.nhm-wien.ac.at/en/narrenturm

THE OTTO WAGNER HOSPITAL

The Otto Wagner Hospital, originally known as "Am Steinhof," occupies a unique place in Vienna's historical and cultural narrative. Situated in the Steinhof area of Vienna's 14th district, this expansive complex represents a striking fusion of architectural ingenuity and a sobering historical legacy. Designed by the iconic architect Otto Wagner, the hospital opened its doors in 1907.

At the time of its inauguration, it was celebrated as one of Europe's most modern and advanced psychiatric institutions. However, the hospital's later role in the atrocities of the Nazi regime casts a long shadow over its storied history, making it a place of both reverence and reflection.

Architectural and Medical Innovation

The hospital's pavilion-style design was groundbreaking for its time. Comprising 60 distinct buildings spread across a sprawling campus, the layout was meticulously planned to provide a tranquil and therapeutic environment for patients. This innovative approach to psychiatric care emphasized the importance of space, light, and individualized treatment, setting a new standard in the field. Each pavilion was tailored to specific patient needs, reflecting the burgeoning belief that architecture could play a vital role in mental health treatment.

Kirche am Steinhof by Otto Wagner (1907)

At the heart of the hospital complex stands the Kirche am Steinhof, a masterpiece of Art Nouveau architecture designed by Otto Wagner himself. The church's golden dome, intricate mosaics, and stained glass windows symbolize hope and healing, offering spiritual solace to patients and visitors alike.

Notably, Wagner also designed a functional restroom within the church to accommodate the needs of patients, a feature that led contemporary critics to label it as the "first atheistic church in the world" in local newspapers of the time. Additionally, the hospital featured an Art Nouveau theater and other cultural amenities, underscoring the holistic vision behind its design.

The Interwar Period: A Changing Role

Following the First World War, the hospital underwent significant changes. The western section, initially designed as a sanatorium for private patients, was repurposed as a pulmonary care center, reflecting the evolving medical needs of the time. Despite these adjustments, the facility remained a cornerstone of psychiatric care in Vienna, continuing to embody the progressive ideals of its founders.

The Nazi Era: A Dark Chapter

The hospital's reputation as a beacon of medical innovation was irreparably tarnished during the Nazi regime. Under the guise of "Aktion T4," the hospital became a site for the systematic murder of individuals deemed "unworthy of life." This program targeted patients classified as "genetically ill," leading to forced sterilizations and mass deportations. Approximately 3,200 patients were transported from the hospital to extermination centers, where they were murdered.

Between the hospital pavilions

The darkest chapter in the hospital's history is linked to Am Spiegelgrund, a children's ward established within the complex. Divided into a reform school and a medical ward, Am Spiegelgrund became a site of unspeakable atrocities. Children with disabilities or considered socially "undesirable" were subjected to medical experiments, starvation, and abuse. Many were killed through lethal injections, gas poisoning, or deliberate neglect. Over 789 children lost their lives in this ward, their deaths recorded as "natural causes" to conceal the truth.

Dr. Heinrich Gross, a leading psychiatrist at Am Spiegelgrund, played a central role in these crimes. Gross conducted experiments on the bodies of murdered children, preserving their brains as "medical specimens." Despite his involvement in these atrocities, Gross evaded justice for decades, even serving as a court psychiatrist in post-war Austria. His actions came to light only in the latter years of his life, prompting widespread outrage and calls for accountability.

Another controversial figure associated with the hospital's history is Hans Asperger. Known for his early research on autism, Asperger referred several children to Am Spiegelgrund, raising questions about his complicity in the Nazi euthanasia program. While his contributions to psychiatry remain significant, his involvement in these dark events has cast a shadow over his legacy.

Memorialization and Modern Use

In the aftermath of World War II, the Otto Wagner Hospital faced the challenge of confronting its past while continuing to serve as a medical facility. Many of its original buildings remain in use, housing various medical departments and research centers. The Kirche am Steinhof continues to stand as a symbol of hope and resilience, attracting visitors with its architectural splendor and historical significance.

Efforts to address the hospital's dark history culminated in the establishment of the Memorial to the History of Nazi Medicine in Vienna, which opened in 2002. This memorial, located within the hospital grounds, serves as a powerful reminder of the atrocities committed there and honors the memory of the victims. Visitors can learn about the history of the "Aktion T4" program, the horrors of Am Spiegelgrund, and the broader implications of Nazi medical practices.

Kirche am Steinhof | Church of St. Leopold

Historical Significance: The Kirche am Steinhof, also known as the Church of St. Leopold, is one of Vienna's most iconic examples of Art Nouveau architecture. Designed by Otto Wagner and consecrated in 1907, the church was built as part of the "Am Steinhof" psychiatric hospital complex. It was specifically intended to serve the spiritual needs of the hospital's patients, blending functionality with architectural beauty. The church's design incorporates innovative features such as wheelchair-accessible ramps and a restroom—a detail that drew criticism in its time, with some dubbing it the "first atheistic church" due to its practicality-focused design. The Kirche am Steinhof is celebrated for its golden dome, intricate mosaics by Koloman Moser, and stained glass windows that depict scenes of healing and hope.

Kirche am Steinhof

Architectural Highlights: The church's layout and design reflect Otto Wagner's commitment to the ideals of the Secessionist movement. The interior features minimalist, yet profoundly symbolic, elements. The use of gold and white throughout the building emphasizes purity and divine light. The altar, surrounded by mosaics of angels and saints, exudes a serene and uplifting atmosphere. The exterior's gilded dome and Jugendstil ornamentation make it a standout feature of the Vienna skyline.

Cultural Impact: The Kirche am Steinhof is not only an architectural masterpiece but also a symbol of Vienna's dedication to holistic healing during the early 20th century. It demonstrates how art, architecture, and medicine were intertwined to create a supportive environment for patients.

Address: Baumgartner Höhe 1, 1140 Vienna

Public transport: U3 to Ottakring, Tram 2 to Baumgarten

Opening hours: The church is open for visits only during the period from March 15, 2025 – October 31, 2025. Visiting hours are as follows:

Tuesday to Friday: 10:00 AM – 5:00 PM

Saturday: 2:00 PM – 5:00 PM

Sunday: 11:00 AM – 5:00 PM

www.wienmuseum.at/otto_wagner_kirche_am_steinhof_en

THE CEMETERY OF THE NAMELESS

Hidden along the quiet banks of the Danube River, far from the grandeur of Vienna's renowned cemeteries like the Zentralfriedhof, lies the *Friedhof der Namenlosen*, or Cemetery of the Nameless. This small, secluded burial ground serves as the final resting place for those denied identity and family recognition in death. The unnamed victims buried here were swept away by the Danube's relentless currents, their bodies washed ashore, and their stories lost to the waters.

While it lacks the prominence of Vienna's historic sites, the *Friedhof der Namenlosen* holds a unique, melancholic significance. Its simple graves and humble markers quietly narrate tragedies of lives cut short—lives that remain nameless. We will explore the history, cultural meaning, and somber atmosphere of the cemetery, which embodies Vienna's nuanced relationship with death, remembrance, and loss.

Origins of the Friedhof der Namenlosen

Nestled in Vienna's Albern district, the cemetery is located along a stretch of the Danube notorious for its treacherous currents. Historically, this area became a somber repository for drowned bodies carried downstream, often from far-off places like Germany or Hungary.

Without documentation or personal belongings to identify them, these victims remained nameless.

The Cemetery of the Nameless

The origins of the cemetery date back to 1840, when local fishermen in Albern began providing burials for the unidentified bodies found along the riverbanks. The first cemetery was a modest plot of land, marked by simple wooden crosses for those whose identities and stories were lost to the Danube.

Flooding repeatedly disrupted the original site, and in 1900, a new cemetery was established on higher ground. This new location, where the cemetery remains today, provided a safer and more permanent resting place for these forgotten souls. Over time, the *Friedhof der Namenlosen* became a poignant symbol of Vienna's care for those who would otherwise be forgotten.

The Cemetery's Layout and Atmosphere

The Friedhof der Namenlosen is a modest, tranquil space, home to approximately 100 graves. Most are marked by weathered wooden crosses, inscribed simply with "Namenlos" (Nameless). On rare occasions, if a victim's identity was later discovered, a name might appear on the marker.

The Chapel at the Cemetery of the Nameless

The cemetery's stark simplicity is its defining feature. A small chapel, built in 1935, stands at the entrance, its quiet presence inviting reflection. Surrounded by trees and removed from the bustling city, the cemetery feels like a world unto itself. The nearby sound of the Danube's flowing waters adds to its contemplative atmosphere, a reminder of the natural forces that shaped the fates of those buried here.

Time has left its mark on the cemetery. The crosses lean gently, weathered and bowed as if yielding to nature's will. Despite its modest size, the Friedhof der Namenlosen is imbued with profound meaning, offering a place for quiet remembrance. Visitors sometimes leave small tributes—flowers, candles, or simple tokens—in honor of those whose names and lives remain unknown.

In its understated way, the Friedhof der Namenlosen is a powerful testament to Vienna's willingness to remember and care for the forgotten. The cemetery's modesty, far from diminishing its impact, reinforces its role as a place of quiet dignity and reflection. Far from Vienna's famous landmarks, it offers an intimate and poignant connection to the city's complex history of life, death, and memory.

Graves without names or dates.

Stories of the Unnamed Dead

One of the most poignant aspects of the *Friedhof der Namenlosen* is the mystery surrounding the lives of those buried there. For most, nothing is known about their identities or the circumstances of their deaths. Many were victims of accidents, suicides, or tragic misfortune. Some were travelers who fell into the river, victims of boat accidents, or individuals attempting to flee political persecution, crossing borders during turbulent periods of European history.

The anonymity of these graves reflects the precariousness of life along the Danube in the 19th and early 20th centuries. Many of the deceased were likely people living on the margins of society—migrants, refugees, the homeless, or the poor. Their deaths speak to the hidden struggles of those who lived near the river or depended on it for their livelihoods, a stark contrast to the opulence often associated with Vienna.

The Nameless Bride

Among the cemetery's many graves, one stands out: that of "The Nameless Bride." Her body was discovered in the late 1800s, washed ashore in a bridal gown, her identity a complete mystery. Her tragic story has become local legend, and she is now a near-mythical figure in Viennese folklore. Visitors often leave flowers on her grave, captivated by the haunting tale of a bride who never reached her wedding day.

The Cemetery of the Nameless

A Place of Remembrance and Ritual

Despite its isolation, the *Friedhof der Namenlosen* holds deep cultural and spiritual significance. Each year, on All Saints' Day (November 1st), the cemetery becomes the focus of a heartfelt memorial service to honor the nameless dead. This tradition, which dates back to the 19th century, sees local fishermen and Albern residents gather to light candles, lay wreaths, and say prayers. The ceremony serves as a poignant reminder of the community's enduring commitment to those who have no family to mourn them.

The cemetery is also steeped in folklore. Its proximity to the Danube—a river entwined with Viennese life—has inspired ghost stories and legends of wandering spirits. The cemetery's remote, melancholic atmosphere amplifies these tales, making it a focal point for supernatural lore.

Over the years, the *Friedhof der Namenlosen* has quietly attracted visitors drawn to its unique history and somber beauty. It has been immortalized in literature, art, and film, becoming a symbol of Vienna's darker, reflective side. Jessie Deeter's documentary *The Dead of the Danube* explores the cemetery's history, bringing its poignant story to a wider audience and shedding light on the lives of the forgotten.

Unlike Vienna's grand cemeteries with their ornate monuments and famous graves, this modest cemetery speaks to the universal dignity of human life. It offers a quiet counterpoint to the imperial splendor of sites like the Hofburg or Schönbrunn Palace, reminding visitors of the city's history of loss and tragedy.

A Place of Solitude and Reflection

The cemetery's remote location adds to its mystique. Accessible only with effort, it offers an escape from Vienna's bustling streets, inviting visitors into a space of introspection and remembrance. The *Friedhof der Namenlosen* is not a major tourist attraction but a solemn place for reflection on the fragility and transience of life.

For those who make the journey, the cemetery offers a glimpse into a forgotten chapter of Viennese history. Its simple crosses and unadorned graves remind us that even the most anonymous lives deserve to be honored.

Friedhof der Namenlosen | Cemetery of the Nameless

Historical Significance: The Friedhof der Namenlosen, or Cemetery of the Nameless, is a poignant and secluded burial site located along the Danube River. Established in the 19th century by local fishermen, it became the final resting place for unidentified victims washed ashore by the river's powerful currents.

Address: Schifffahrtsstraße 2, 1110 Vienna

Public transport: U3 to Enkplatz > Bus 76A to Albern Hafen

Opening hours: Accessible daily; no fixed opening hours

Online: Not available

VIENNA IN THE GREAT WAR

The Great War, known later as World War I, profoundly shaped Europe and the world. At the heart of this massive conflict stood Vienna, the capital of the Austro-Hungarian Empire. A cultural and intellectual hub before the war, Vienna faced immense transformation as it transitioned from being the opulent seat of a vast, multi-ethnic empire to a city on the edge of collapse. This essay delves into Vienna's experience during the war, from the political climate leading up to 1914, through the socioeconomic strains and the eventual disintegration of the empire, to the legacy of the war on the city and its people.

Vienna on the Eve of the War

At the start of the 20th century, Vienna was one of the great cities of Europe. As the capital of the Austro-Hungarian Empire, it was a major cultural, artistic, and political center. The city's cosmopolitan nature reflected the diversity of the empire itself, which spanned a vast area of Central Europe and included various nationalities: Austrians, Hungarians, Czechs, Poles, Serbs, Croats, Slovenes, Romanians, Italians, and others. This melting pot of cultures made Vienna a city of rich artistic innovation, where figures like Gustav Klimt, Egon Schiele, and Sigmund Freud thrived.

One month after the Sarajevo assassination, Franz Joseph issued the To My Peoples! (An Meine Völker!) declaration at Schönbrunn Palace, formally announcing the Monarchy's declaration of war against Serbia.

However, despite its cultural vitality, Vienna was also a city under strain. The empire's political structure was creaking under the weight of nationalism, ethnic tensions, and the increasing demands for autonomy from various subject peoples. The assassination of Archduke Franz Ferdinand, the heir to the Austro-Hungarian throne, in Sarajevo on June 28, 1914, by a Serbian nationalist, set off a chain of events that would drag Europe into war. While the assassination took place far from Vienna, its effects reverberated through the city and across the empire.

The Outbreak of War and Vienna's Initial Enthusiasm

When Austria-Hungary declared war on Serbia in late July 1914, it set into motion a web of alliances that quickly expanded the conflict into a full-scale world war. Initially, there was a sense of patriotic fervor in Vienna. Like much of Europe, the citizens of the empire were swept up in the excitement of war, with many believing it would be a short conflict. Parades filled the streets, soldiers marched off to the front, and the idea of a swift victory united much of the city.

Vienna, being far from the front lines, was not immediately affected by the war in a direct military sense. However, this initial enthusiasm quickly gave way to the grim realities of a protracted conflict.

Economic Hardship and Social Unrest

As the war dragged on, Vienna began to feel the strain of prolonged conflict. The Austro-Hungarian Empire was not as industrialized as its German ally or the Western powers, and it struggled to supply its military forces with the necessary resources. The city's industries were gradually converted to support the war effort, but the economic foundations of the empire were inadequate for the scale of the conflict.

Food shortages became a major issue in Vienna by 1916. The city's population, already burdened by a slow pre-war economy, now faced widespread hunger, exacerbated by poor harvests, the requisitioning of supplies for the military, and the disruption of trade routes. Bread lines grew longer, and inflation soared, reducing the purchasing power of ordinary citizens.

Women took on new roles in the workforce as men went to the front, and the social fabric of the city shifted. This transition placed significant stress on families and society, with many women left to manage households with little income or support. The war also saw the arrival of thousands of refugees from the eastern front, which added further pressure on the city's resources and services.

Social unrest became more pronounced as the war dragged on. Vienna's diverse population, once united in support of the war effort, became increasingly fragmented. Ethnic tensions that had simmered before the war intensified, as the various nationalities within the empire began to question their loyalty to a crumbling Habsburg regime. Political movements, such as socialism and nationalism, gained ground as the war's cost in lives and resources mounted.

The Front Line at Home: The Impact on Daily Life

While the physical destruction of war was largely absent from Vienna, the psychological toll on its citizens was immense. As news from the front grew ever more grim, with heavy losses in battles like the Isonzo offensives and the Brusilov Offensive, the morale of the city's residents began to collapse. Military defeats, coupled with food shortages, further eroded public confidence in the monarchy.

The city was filled with hospitals to treat the wounded, and more and more soldiers returned as disabled veterans, visible reminders of the horrors of the front. The contrast between the opulence of pre-war Vienna and the suffering of the war years was stark. Buildings once known for hosting grand events and concerts were converted into makeshift care facilities, while the war economy left many unemployed or destitute.

The Imperial War Ministry on the Ring.

The Collapse of the Empire and the War's End

By 1917, the situation had become untenable. The Russian Revolution in the east gave hope to socialist movements in Vienna, who sought an end to the war and relief from economic deprivation. Emperor Karl I, who ascended to the throne in 1916 following the death of Emperor Franz Joseph, attempted to negotiate a peace, but the war continued.

As Austria-Hungary's military situation deteriorated, so too did the empire's internal cohesion. Ethnic groups began to declare independence, and the empire rapidly disintegrated. By November 1918, the Austro-Hungarian Empire was effectively no more, and Vienna's place at the heart of a vast, multi-ethnic realm was replaced by its new role as the capital of a small, German-speaking republic.

The war officially ended on November 11, 1918, but for Vienna, the aftermath was one of political turmoil, economic hardship, and profound social change. The Treaty of Saint-Germain, signed in 1919, formalized the dissolution of the Austro-Hungarian Empire and imposed harsh conditions on Austria, including the loss of significant territory. Vienna, once a grand imperial capital, now found itself as the center of a much-reduced state, surrounded by new national borders that cut it off from its traditional economic hinterlands.

Legacy of the War on Vienna

The Great War left an indelible mark on Vienna. Politically, it marked the end of the Habsburg dynasty and the centuries-old Austro-Hungarian Empire, reshaping Central Europe's political landscape. The new Republic of Austria was left economically weak and politically divided, with its capital Vienna struggling to adjust to its reduced status.

Culturally, the war's aftermath saw Vienna become a center for new movements in art, literature, and philosophy. The psychological trauma of the war influenced many intellectuals and artists, giving rise to movements like Expressionism and contributing to the psychoanalytic work of figures like Sigmund Freud. However, the city's cultural dynamism was tempered by the extreme poverty and political instability that followed the war, setting the stage for the tensions that would erupt in the interwar years.

Vienna's experience during the Great War was one of transformation and loss. The war brought about the end of the Austro-Hungarian Empire, and with it, Vienna's position as a major imperial capital.

Museum of Military History

Heeresgeschichtliches Museum | Military History Museum

Historical Significance: The Heeresgeschichtliches Museum is Austria's premier museum dedicated to military history. It houses artifacts from the Ottoman Wars, the Napoleonic Wars, the Austro-Hungarian Empire, and both World Wars. The museum is located in the historic Arsenal complex and includes key exhibits such as the car in which Archduke Franz Ferdinand was assassinated, an event that triggered World War I.

Address: Arsenal, Objekt 1, 1030 Vienna

Public transport: Tram D to Heeresgeschichtliches Museum

Opening hours: Daily: 9 a.m. – 5 p.m.; Closed on Mondays

Online: https://www.hgm.at

SIGMUND FREUD IN VIENNA

Vienna was home to one of the greatest minds of the 20th century—Dr. Sigmund Freud. The "father of psychoanalysis" spent many of his most productive years in Vienna, living and working at Berggasse 19, in the city's Ninth District. His home and practice became a center for groundbreaking ideas that transformed our understanding of the human mind.

Freud's daily routine, unwavering in its structure, was a testament to his disciplined intellect and his fascination with the human psyche. But what truly set Freud apart was his fearless exploration into the darker recesses of the human mind. He delved deeper into the hidden layers of human behavior, desires, and fears than anyone before him, unraveling the mysteries of the unconscious, neurosis, and repressed emotions. This essay takes you on a journey through a typical day in the life of Professor Freud in Vienna, from his morning rituals to his evening reflections, and his unprecedented dive into the shadows of human nature.

Morning Rituals: The Start of the Day

At exactly seven in the morning, Freud's day began, and he was nothing if not meticulous in maintaining his routine. Every morning, a housemaid would prepare a hot bath for him, and lay out a fresh suit that carried the familiar scent of cigar smoke—an aroma that would follow him throughout his day. His breakfast was always the same: a soft-boiled egg and steak tartare, served with unwavering consistency. Freud cherished this predictability, which allowed him to focus his energies on his patients and research.

The entrance to Freud's apartment and office, which are now part of a museum.

Shortly after his bath, Freud's barber would arrive to trim his beard and comb his hair—another daily ritual that reflected his commitment to order and appearance. By eight a.m., Freud was ready to start his professional day. From then until noon, he received patients in his consulting room, a space filled with artifacts that gave his practice a unique atmosphere.

The Consultation Room: A Sanctuary of Ancient Gods and Psychoanalysis

Stepping into Freud's consultation room was like entering a sacred space. The waiting and consulting rooms were filled with ancient artifacts, collected with a passion that rivaled his work in psychoanalysis. Freud was an avid collector of antique sculptures, vases, tombstones, and other archaeological treasures from ancient Egypt, Greece, and Rome. His collection included over 3,000 objects, turning his home into something of a private museum.

These "old and dirty gods," as Freud affectionately called them, were more than decorative pieces. They symbolized the human preoccupation with death, love, and the mysteries of existence—concepts that Freud would explore in his psychoanalytic theories. The mythical figures in his collection were omnipresent, watching over his patients as they waited for their appointments, as if reminding them that they, too, were grappling with timeless human struggles.

Freud once confided in his friend, the writer Stefan Zweig, that his passion for collecting antiquities had become almost as time-consuming and expensive as his work in psychoanalysis. He often admitted to spending more time reading books on archaeology than on psychology. The significance of these artifacts in his life mirrored his belief that the human mind was an ancient structure, layered with historical and emotional sediment that required careful excavation.

As patients lay down on the iconic couch, they were not alone in sharing their deepest fears, dreams, and desires. They were accompanied by Freud's dog, a Chow Chow who often sat nearby. Freud trusted the instincts of his dog so much that he believed her reactions to new patients could reveal their true psychological state. "The dog is never mistaken," he once wrote, underscoring the connection between his psychoanalytic insights and his keen observations of animal behavior.

The Afternoon Walk: A Stroll Through Vienna's History

By noon, Freud had finished his morning appointments, and it was time for lunch. His family, including his wife Martha, his sister-in-law Minna, and his daughter Anna, all gathered promptly for the meal.

Family dinners were an integral part of Freud's routine, a time when his work was momentarily set aside in favor of familial connection.

After lunch, Freud would embark on his daily walk—a ritual that served both for digestion and reflection. He would make his way up the incline of Berggasse, accompanied by his trusty canine companion. Their path took them along Währingerstrasse and Schwarzspanierstrasse, where they would pass by the house at number 15, where Beethoven had died decades earlier. Freud, despite his admiration for many art forms, had little interest in music and was largely indifferent to Beethoven's legacy. His thoughts were occupied with more pressing matters—those of the human mind.

Freud's walk culminated at the meadow in front of the Votive Church, a favorite spot for his dog to play. After the short respite, Freud would return home, ready to face the patients awaiting him for the afternoon session.

Evening Reflections: Freud's Love for Sherlock Holmes

As dusk settled over Vienna, Freud's day of consultations came to an end. Dinner would often feature one of his favorite dishes—Italian artichokes, Tafelspitz (boiled beef), or Viennese onion roast—prepared with care. But Freud's day was far from over. After the meal, he would go for another walk, this time alone, retracing his steps from earlier in the day. His path led him past familiar landmarks, such as the university, the Burgtheater, and Beethoven's Pasqualatihaus, until he reached Café Landmann.

It was in the subdued atmosphere of Café Landmann that Freud found peace. There, surrounded by the murmurs of Vienna's intellectual elite, he would light his twentieth cigar of the day, sip his coffee, and let the day's events fade into the background. Freud's appreciation for coffee houses was rooted in their role as cultural hubs, places where one could be alone with one's thoughts while surrounded by the hum of conversation.

Café Landtmann

Returning home, Freud would spend his final hours of the day in quiet solitude. His preferred way to unwind was by reading detective stories, particularly those of Sherlock Holmes. Freud, much like the fictional detective, possessed an unparalleled ability to unravel mysteries—only his cases dealt with the human psyche rather than crime. As he read, Freud would often anticipate the plot twists, confidently identifying the murderer long before the story revealed it.

Legacy and Final Days in Vienna

Freud's days in Vienna were numbered as political tensions grew in Europe. In 1938, the Anschluss brought the Nazi regime to Austria, and Freud, a Jewish intellectual, was no longer safe in the city he had called home for over five decades. With the help of influential friends, including the psychoanalyst Marie Bonaparte, Freud fled Vienna for London, where he would live out the final year of his life.

Despite his forced exile, Freud's legacy remains indelibly tied to Vienna. His former home at Berggasse 19 is now the Sigmund Freud

Museum, where visitors can explore the rooms that once housed his groundbreaking theories and collections. The museum stands as a testament to Freud's enduring influence on psychology, culture, and the way we understand ourselves.

In retracing Freud's steps, both literal and intellectual, one gains insight into a mind that sought to unravel the deepest mysteries of human behavior. From his meticulously structured days to his unwavering dedication to psychoanalysis, Freud's life in Vienna continues to captivate those who walk through the city's streets, imagining the world as the professor once saw it.

Sigmund Freud Museum

Historical Significance: The Sigmund Freud Museum is located in the apartment where Sigmund Freud lived and worked from 1891 to 1938, before fleeing to London.

Address: Berggasse 19, 1090 Vienna

Public transport: U2, U4 to Schottenring or Tram D to Schlickgasse

Opening hours: Daily: 10 a.m. – 6 p.m.

Online: www.freud-museum.at

Café Landtmann

Historical Significance: Established in 1873, Café Landtmann is one of Vienna's most iconic coffeehouses and was frequented by famous figures such as Sigmund Freud, Marlene Dietrich, and Gustav Mahler.

Address: Universitätsring 4, 1010 Vienna

Public transport: U2 to Schottentor or Tram 1, 71, D to Rathausplatz/Burgtheater

Opening hours: Daily: 7:30 a.m. – 11 p.m.

Online: www.landtmann.at

THE DARK HISTORY OF JUDENPLATZ

Judenplatz, located in the heart of Vienna's first district, stands today as a haunting reminder of the city's complex and often tragic relationship with its Jewish community. Over the centuries, Vienna has been a center of intellectual, artistic, and cultural development, but it has also been a place of religious persecution, prejudice, and violence. One of the darkest chapters in this history is the series of pogroms and anti-Semitic violence that repeatedly devastated Vienna's Jewish population. These pogroms, culminating in the horrors of the Holocaust, are memorialized today at Judenplatz, a site of both destruction and remembrance.

This essay explores the history of Jewish pogroms in Vienna, focusing on the events that took place around Judenplatz, and examining the long-standing tension between the Jewish community and the broader society. The memorials that now stand at Judenplatz not only commemorate the suffering and loss of life but also serve as a testament to the resilience of Vienna's Jewish community, which has survived centuries of persecution.

The Holocaust Memorial at Judenplatz

Early Jewish Presence in Vienna

The Jewish presence in Vienna dates back to at least the 12th century, when the first significant Jewish community established itself in the city. Jews were drawn to Vienna due to its position as a major European trade hub and the relative tolerance of the ruling powers during certain periods. This early community flourished in what is now known as Judenplatz, which became the center of Jewish life in medieval Vienna. The Jewish population of the time was involved in trade, finance, and scholarship, and they contributed significantly to the city's economy.

Despite their contributions, Jews in Vienna, as elsewhere in Europe, lived under precarious conditions. They were subject to strict regulations and were often marginalized by the Christian majority. Anti-Semitic sentiments were deeply ingrained in medieval Christian society, fueled by religious prejudice and economic envy. Jews were blamed for a variety of societal ills, ranging from the Black Death to economic downturns. This tension set the stage for the violent pogroms that would follow.

The First Pogrom: 1420-1421

One of the earliest and most devastating attacks on Vienna's Jewish population occurred in the early 15th century, during what is now known as the *Wiener Gesera* (Vienna Edict). In 1420, Duke Albert V of Austria, influenced by growing anti-Semitic fervor and indebted to Jewish moneylenders, issued a decree accusing the Jewish community of heresy and ritual murder—a common but baseless accusation known as the *blood libel*. The duke ordered the arrest of all Jews in Vienna and the confiscation of their property.

In 1421, the situation escalated into a full-scale pogrom. The Jewish population of Vienna was rounded up, and many were imprisoned or tortured. Some were forcibly converted to Christianity, while others were executed. The Jewish community's synagogues and homes were destroyed, including the great synagogue that once stood at Judenplatz. This violent expulsion effectively wiped out the Jewish presence in Vienna for almost a century, marking the first major pogrom in the city's history.

The remains of the synagogue, rediscovered in the 20th century, now lie beneath Judenplatz and are a part of the memorial complex dedicated to the memory of the Jewish community that once thrived there.

Jewish Return and the Second Pogrom: 1670

After their expulsion in 1421, Jews were gradually allowed to return to Vienna during the 16th century, although they remained subject to strict regulations. By the mid-17th century, a new Jewish community had developed in the Leopoldstadt district, across the Danube River from the city center. This community, like its predecessor, contributed to Vienna's economy and culture but remained vulnerable to anti-Semitic violence.

In 1670, Vienna experienced another devastating pogrom under the rule of Emperor Leopold I. The emperor, influenced by his anti-Semitic Spanish wife and pressured by the Catholic Church, ordered the expulsion of all Jews from Vienna. The Jewish population, which had grown to several thousand, was forced to leave the city, and their homes and synagogues were destroyed once again. This event marked another dark chapter in Vienna's history of Jewish persecution, leaving the Jewish community in a state of vulnerability and disarray.

The Enlightenment and Jewish Integration

Despite these violent episodes, the Jewish community in Vienna gradually began to recover, particularly during the reign of Emperor Joseph II in the late 18th century. Joseph II, a key figure of the Enlightenment, introduced a series of reforms known as the *Edicts of Tolerance*, which aimed to grant greater rights and freedoms to religious minorities, including Jews. These reforms allowed Jews to engage in certain professions, attend universities, and live in the city without fear of expulsion.

By the 19th century, Vienna's Jewish community had once again become an integral part of the city's social, cultural, and economic life. Jewish intellectuals, artists, and financiers played crucial roles in the development of modern Vienna, contributing to its reputation as a center of creativity and innovation. Figures such as Sigmund Freud, Theodor Herzl, and Gustav Mahler were all part of Vienna's Jewish intellectual elite, helping to shape the city's intellectual and cultural landscape.

However, despite these advances, anti-Semitism remained deeply rooted in Viennese society, particularly in the political arena. The rise of nationalist and populist movements in the late 19th century, most notably led by the anti-Semitic mayor Karl Lueger, foreshadowed the horrors that would befall the Jewish community in the 20th century.

The Holocaust and the Destruction of Vienna's Jews

The darkest chapter in Vienna's history of Jewish persecution came with the rise of the Nazis in the 1930s and the subsequent annexation of Austria by Nazi Germany in 1938, known as the *Anschluss*. The Jewish population of Vienna at the time numbered around 200,000, one of the largest Jewish communities in Europe.

The "Stones of Remembrance" are small memorial plaques embedded in the ground at the former residences of deported Jewish residents of Vienna.

Following the Anschluss, Vienna's Jewish community was subjected to a brutal campaign of terror, forced deportations, and mass murder. Jewish businesses were looted during Kristallnacht in November 1938, and Jewish families were evicted from their homes. Many Jews were sent to concentration camps, while others were forced to emigrate. Those who could not escape were eventually deported to extermination camps such as Auschwitz, where they perished in the Holocaust.

By the end of World War II, more than 65,000 Austrian Jews, including the vast majority of Vienna's Jewish population, had been murdered in the Holocaust. The Jewish presence in Vienna, which had existed for centuries, was all but eradicated.

Beneath Judenplatz, the excavated remains of the medieval synagogue destroyed in the 1421 pogrom are displayed in the Judenplatz Museum. This underground memorial connects the pogroms of the past with the horrors of the Holocaust, creating a continuity of remembrance that stretches across centuries of persecution.

Jüdisches Museum Wien – Dorotheergasse | Jewish Museum Vienna – Dorotheergasse

Historical Significance: The Jewish Museum Vienna provides a comprehensive overview of Jewish history, culture, and life in Austria, with a focus on Vienna. It features permanent and temporary exhibitions that cover the Jewish community's contributions to the city's development as well as the tragic impact of the Holocaust. The museum is split across two locations, including one at Judenplatz, which highlights the medieval Jewish heritage of the city.

Address: Dorotheergasse 11, 1010 Vienna

Public transport: U3 to Stephansplatz; U1 to Karlsplatz

Opening hours: Daily: 10 a.m. – 6 p.m.; Closed on Saturdays

Online: www.jmw.at

Jüdisches Museum Wien – Judenplatz | Jewish Museum Vienna – Judenplatz

Historical Significance: The Judenplatz location of the Jewish Museum Vienna focuses on the rich medieval Jewish history of Vienna. It houses exhibitions about the Jewish community's life in the Middle Ages and features the remains of a medieval synagogue. The site also includes the Judenplatz Holocaust Memorial, which commemorates the Austrian Jewish victims of the Holocaust, serving as a reminder of the community's tragic fate during World War II.

Address: Judenplatz 8, 1010 Vienna

Public transport: U1, U3 to Stephansplatz; Tram 1, 71, D to Rathausplatz/Burgtheater

Opening hours: Daily: 10 a.m. – 6 p.m.; Closed on Saturdays

Online: www.jmw.at

NAZI ERA: LOCATIONS OF CRIMES AND MEMORIALS

Vienna, a city known for its cultural and intellectual achievements, was tragically entangled in the horrors of the Nazi regime. After the Anschluss in 1938, when Austria was annexed to Nazi Germany, Vienna became a key location for the Third Reich's plans, serving as both a hub of Nazi ideology and a site of atrocities. The dark legacy of this time is marked across the city in locations where crimes were committed and memorials where the victims of this brutal period are remembered.

The Anschluss, the annexation of Austria into Nazi Germany, occurred on March 12, 1938, and transformed Vienna from a culturally rich city into a vital center for Nazi administration. For many Austrians, the Anschluss was initially met with celebration, but for Jews, political dissidents, and other marginalized groups, it marked the beginning of persecution, deportation, and extermination.

After the annexation, Vienna became a hotspot for Nazi administration, and the once cosmopolitan city fell under the grip of totalitarianism. The Gestapo, the Nazi secret police, quickly established their headquarters in the city at the former Hotel Métropole, turning it into a place of fear and torture. The Nazis' brutal policies soon turned the city's streets into sites of terror, where Jews were publicly humiliated and thousands of citizens were arrested, interrogated, and often murdered.

Locations of Crimes

Hitler's Balcony: One of the most infamous sites in Vienna's Nazi history is the balcony of the Neue Burg, a wing of the Hofburg Palace, from which Adolf Hitler addressed a massive crowd on March 15, 1938. This event is deeply ingrained in Austrian and world history as it marked the official proclamation of the Anschluss, the annexation of Austria into Nazi Germany. This moment symbolized the country's descent into the horrors of totalitarianism, anti-Semitic persecution, and war. The balcony itself has become a grim reminder of Vienna's involvement in the Nazi regime, a place where a dark chapter of history was written.

The Anschluss and Hitler's Speech: After the annexation of Austria, Hitler arrived in Vienna to a hero's welcome, a moment that remains controversial due to the enthusiastic reception he received from a significant portion of the Austrian population. On March 15, 1938, just days after German troops marched into Austria, Hitler stood on the balcony of the Neue Burg and addressed a cheering crowd estimated to be around 200,000 people. The square below was filled with Austrians who came to hear their new Führer.

Hitler's Balcony (Neue Burg) Hofburg Palace.

In this speech, Hitler declared that Austria was now part of the German Reich, effectively ending Austria's independence and integrating it into the Third Reich. The speech was a propaganda moment, signaling the success of the Anschluss and reinforcing Nazi ideals. It also marked the beginning of systematic persecution of Jews, dissidents, and other groups deemed undesirable by the regime.

Significance of the Balcony: This balcony, although architecturally unremarkable, became a powerful symbol of Nazi domination over Austria. From this very spot, Hitler declared the end of Austria as a sovereign state and the absorption of the country into Nazi Germany. It was a moment that sealed the fate of hundreds of thousands of Austrian Jews and other minorities who would soon face deportation, persecution, and extermination.

The day after Hitler's speech, Jews in Vienna were publicly humiliated, beaten, and forced to scrub the streets while jeering crowds watched. This public humiliation and degradation of the Jewish community foreshadowed the mass arrests, deportations, and murders that would follow in the coming years. Vienna's Jewish population, which numbered over 200,000 in 1938, was decimated by the Holocaust.

Nazi Crimes Associated with the Site: While the balcony itself did not witness physical violence, it served as the platform for a speech that legitimized Nazi crimes in Austria. The Anschluss led to the rapid imposition of Nazi policies in Vienna, including the Aryanization of Jewish businesses, the expulsion of Jewish professionals from their jobs, and the seizure of property. Jewish Austrians were quickly stripped of their rights, livelihoods, and eventually, their lives.

The proclamation from this balcony was not just a symbolic moment; it was the beginning of an era of systemic atrocities. The speech marked the official start of the integration of Austria into Nazi Germany and the extension of the Holocaust into Austrian society. Thousands of Austrians would later be deported from sites like the Aspangbahnhof to concentration camps and extermination camps across Europe.

On the site of today's residential building stood the Hotel Metropol until the end of World War II.

Hotel Métropole (Morzinplatz)

One of the most notorious locations in Vienna during the Nazi regime was the Gestapo headquarters at Hotel Métropole on Morzinplatz. The luxurious hotel was converted into a base for the Gestapo soon after the Anschluss. Here, political dissidents, Jews, Roma, and other groups targeted by the regime were brought for interrogation, torture, and often execution.

The building became synonymous with fear, and many Viennese citizens disappeared after being taken there. Today, the site no longer hosts the original building, as it was heavily damaged during World War II and demolished after the war. However, a memorial stands in its place, dedicated to the thousands who suffered at the hands of the Gestapo.

Aspangbahnhof

Aspangbahnhof was a train station from which tens of thousands of Jews were deported to concentration camps, primarily in Poland. Between 1939 and 1942, more than 47,000 Austrian Jews were deported from this station to ghettos and extermination camps in the East. Most of those deported were sent to death camps such as Sobibor, Treblinka, and Auschwitz, where almost none survived. .

Wiener Stadttempel (City Temple)

The Wiener Stadttempel, Vienna's main synagogue, was one of the few Jewish places of worship that survived the November 1938 Kristallnacht pogrom, where Nazis attacked and destroyed Jewish synagogues, businesses, and homes across Austria and Germany. This synagogue survived largely due to its location in a residential building that could not be set on fire without endangering the entire neighborhood. Nevertheless, Vienna's Jewish community suffered tremendously during the pogrom, and many members of the congregation were arrested and deported shortly thereafter. Today, the Stadttempel is a functioning synagogue and an important symbol of Jewish survival in the city. The nearby Holocaust memorial serves as a reminder of the lives lost during this tragic time.

Prater and other Forced Labor Sites

Vienna also saw the exploitation of forced labor under the Nazi regime. Large sections of the city, including the famous Prater park, were used for forced labor by Jews, political prisoners, and others considered enemies of the Reich. Thousands of prisoners were forced to work under brutal conditions, building fortifications, producing weapons, or working in factories essential to the Nazi war effort. In the Prater and elsewhere in Vienna, these individuals faced inhumane treatment and many died from the harsh conditions, starvation, or violence inflicted upon them by their captors. Today, plaques and small memorials across the city, including in the Prater, commemorate the victims of forced labor.

Memorials to the Victims of Nazi Crimes

Judenplatz Holocaust Memorial

One of the most significant memorials in Vienna is the Judenplatz Holocaust Memorial, also known as the *Nameless Library*. Designed by British artist Rachel Whiteread and unveiled in 2000, the memorial is a stark and powerful symbol of the 65,000 Austrian Jews murdered in the Holocaust. The structure, built in the form of a concrete library with books facing inward, symbolizes the vast number of lives lost, as well as the intellectual and cultural contributions erased by the Nazi genocide. The names of the concentration camps where Austrian Jews perished are inscribed at the base of the memorial, and it stands as a permanent reminder of the city's dark past.

Beneath Judenplatz lies a subterranean museum that explores the history of Vienna's Jewish community, which dates back to the Middle Ages. Visitors can also see the remains of a medieval synagogue, uncovered during excavations for the memorial.

Memorial to the Austrian Resistance (Morzinplatz)

On Morzinplatz, the site of the former Gestapo headquarters, stands a monument dedicated to the Austrian resistance movement and the many who perished in their efforts to fight the Nazi regime. The monument, erected in 1968, is simple yet powerful, with an inscription that reads: *"For Freedom, Justice, and Democracy, Never Again Fascism, Millions of Dead Warn Us."* This memorial pays homage to those who resisted the Nazi occupation of Austria, many of whom were arrested, tortured, and executed for their efforts.

Monument against War and Fascism

Monument against War and Fascism (Albertinaplatz)

Another prominent memorial in Vienna is the *Monument against War and Fascism* located in Albertinaplatz. Created by sculptor Alfred Hrdlicka and unveiled in 1988, the monument consists of several sculptural pieces that collectively represent the suffering endured under the Nazi regime. One of the most poignant aspects of the monument is the *Gate of Violence*, which references the victims of war, concentration camps, and forced labor. The monument also features a representation of a hunched-over figure, symbolizing the humiliation and degradation suffered by Jewish citizens forced to scrub the streets during the Anschluss.

Stolpersteine (Stumbling Stones)

Throughout Vienna's streets, Stolpersteine, or "stumbling stones," serve as subtle yet moving reminders of the individuals who were deported and murdered during the Holocaust. These small brass plaques, embedded in the pavement outside the homes of victims, bear the names, dates of birth, and details of their deportation and deaths. Created by artist Gunter Demnig, the Stolpersteine initiative stretches across Europe, reminding passersby of the human lives lost in the Holocaust. Each Stolperstein commemorates a single person, and the act of physically stumbling upon these memorials in everyday life creates a personal connection to the past.

The Deserters Memorial (Ballhausplatz)

Located in Ballhausplatz, this monument was erected in 2014 to commemorate Austrian soldiers who refused to serve in the Wehrmacht during World War II. These individuals were labeled traitors and often executed for their refusal to fight for the Nazi regime. The monument takes the form of a large stone disk with the words *"All Alone"* engraved upon it, symbolizing the isolation and courage of those who resisted the Nazis from within. It serves as a reminder that resistance came in many forms and that not all Austrians supported the fascist regime.

Neue Burg | Hofburg

Historical Significance: The Neue Burg is part of the Hofburg Palace complex in Vienna and stands as a monumental example of late Historicism. Completed in 1913, it was envisioned as part of a grand imperial forum, though the full plan was never realized. Today, it houses several museums, including the Austrian National Library's Papyrus Museum, the Ephesos Museum, and the Weltmuseum Wien. The Neue Burg also features the balcony where Adolf Hitler proclaimed Austria's annexation into Nazi Germany in 1938, making it a site of profound historical importance.

Address: Heldenplatz, 1010 Vienna

Public transport: U3 to Herrengasse, Tram D, 1, 2 to Burgring

Opening hours: Museums: Daily: 10 a.m. – 6 p.m.

www.khm.at/en/visit/collections/ephesos-museum/

Hotel Métropole | Morzinplatz

Historical Significance: The Hotel Métropole, once a grand luxury hotel, stood at Morzinplatz in Vienna until its destruction at the end of World War II. During the Nazi regime, it was repurposed as the headquarters of the Gestapo, serving as a site of terror and persecution. Many prisoners were detained, tortured, and interrogated here. The building was demolished after the war, and today a memorial stands on the site to honor the victims of Nazi oppression.

Address: Morzinplatz, 1010 Vienna

Public transport: U1, U4 to Schwedenplatz

Opening hours: Memorial accessible 24 hours daily

Wiener Stadttempel | City Temple

Historical Significance: The Wiener Stadttempel is the main synagogue in Vienna and the only one that survived the Kristallnacht pogrom of 1938 intact. Built in 1826 by architect Joseph Kornhäusel, the temple was designed in Biedermeier style and concealed within a residential building, as public synagogues were not permitted at the time. Today, it serves as a place of worship and a poignant reminder of Vienna's Jewish heritage and resilience.

Address: Seitenstettengasse 4, 1010 Vienna

Public transport: U1, U4 to Schwedenplatz; U3 to Stephansplatz

Opening hours: Guided tours by appointment

Online: www.ikg-wien.at

Prater

Historical Significance: The Prater is one of Vienna's most iconic attractions, offering a blend of historical charm and modern entertainment. Originally a royal hunting ground, it was opened to the public in 1766 by Emperor Joseph II. Today, it is home to the famous Wurstelprater amusement park, featuring the historic Wiener Riesenrad Ferris wheel, built in 1897. The Prater also includes expansive green spaces, ideal for walking, cycling, and relaxation, as well as restaurants and cultural attractions.

Address: Prater, 1020 Vienna

Public transport: U1, U2 to Praterstern

Opening hours: Park: Open 24 hours daily; Wurstelprater: Seasonal, hours vary

Memorial to the Austrian Resistance | Morzinplatz

Historical Significance: This memorial stands on the site of the former Hotel Métropole, which was used as the Gestapo headquarters during World War II. The monument honors the Austrian resistance fighters who opposed Nazi oppression and serves as a reminder of the atrocities committed during the regime. The design features inscriptions commemorating the victims and celebrating the courage of those who fought for freedom.

Address: Morzinplatz, 1010 Vienna

Public transport: U1, U4 to Schwedenplatz

Opening hours: Accessible 24 hours daily

Judenplatz Holocaust Memorial

Historical Significance: The Judenplatz Holocaust Memorial, also known as the "Nameless Library," was unveiled in 2000 to commemorate the 65,000 Austrian Jews murdered during the Holocaust. Designed by British artist Rachel Whiteread, the memorial resembles an inverted library with spines of books turned inward, symbolizing the untold stories of the victims. Located at Judenplatz, it stands as a poignant reminder of Vienna's Jewish history and the atrocities committed during the Nazi era. Below the square is the Museum Judenplatz, which provides further insight into the Jewish community's history in Vienna.

Address: Judenplatz, 1010 Vienna

Public transport: U1, U3 to Stephansplatz; Tram 1, 71, D to Schwedenplatz

Opening hours: Accessible 24 hours daily (Museum Judenplatz: hours vary)

Online: www.jmw.at

The Deserters Memorial | Ballhausplatz

Historical Significance: The Deserters Memorial at Ballhausplatz honors Austrian soldiers who refused to fight for the Nazi regime during World War II. Installed in 2014, the minimalist stone sculpture, inscribed with "all those who refused to kill," serves as a tribute to these individuals' moral courage and resistance to fascism. The memorial challenges historical narratives that once condemned deserters and instead recognizes them as heroes of conscience.

Address: Ballhausplatz, 1010 Vienna

Public transport: U3 to Herrengasse; Tram 1, D to Burgring

Opening hours: Accessible 24 hours daily

THE FLAK TOWERS

Amid the grandeur and elegance of Vienna's historic streets lie grim remnants of a more sinister chapter in the city's history. The Flak Towers, colossal concrete structures rising from the urban landscape, are stark reminders of the terror and devastation wrought during World War II. Built under the Nazi regime, these towers were intended as both defensive fortifications and propaganda statements. Today, they stand as unsettling monuments to Vienna's role in one of humanity's darkest periods.

Instead of removing these symbols of war, the Austrian authorities opted to repurpose some of them. The tower in Stiftskaserne became a military storage facility, while the one in Arenbergpark was left largely unused. In Augarten, one of the towers now houses a museum, an attempt to integrate the structure into Vienna's modern identity. However, these efforts remain controversial, as many view the towers as enduring symbols of oppression and suffering.

Monuments to a Dark Past

Amid the grandeur and elegance of Vienna's historic streets lie grim remnants of a more sinister chapter in the city's history. The Flak Towers, colossal concrete structures rising from the urban landscape, are stark reminders of the terror and devastation wrought during World War II. Built under the Nazi regime, these towers were intended as both defensive fortifications and propaganda statements. Today, they stand as unsettling monuments to Vienna's role in one of humanity's darkest periods.

The Flak Tower in Augarten

The Rise of the Flak Towers

The Flak Towers were constructed in response to the growing threat of Allied air raids during World War II. After the devastating bombing of Berlin in 1940, Adolf Hitler ordered the construction of massive anti-aircraft towers (Flaktürme) to protect key German cities, including Vienna, Berlin, and Hamburg. Vienna, a city of immense strategic and symbolic importance to the Third Reich, was chosen to house three sets of these formidable structures.

Construction began in 1942, utilizing forced labor from concentration camps and prisoners of war. The towers were built in pairs, with a G-Tower (gun tower) and an L-Tower (leadership or command tower) working in tandem. Each pair formed a fortified complex equipped with anti-aircraft guns capable of firing at high altitudes to target Allied bombers. These towers were also equipped with radar systems, ammunition storage, and even hospitals and civilian shelters, theoretically capable of housing thousands during air raids.

Architectural Brutality

The Flak Towers are among the most imposing examples of Nazi-era architecture. The G-Towers, in particular, are massive, with walls up to 3.5 meters thick and heights exceeding 50 meters. Their brutalist design served a dual purpose: practicality in defense and psychological intimidation. The sheer scale of these structures symbolized the supposed invincibility of the Third Reich. They were constructed to withstand both bombing and siege, standing as fortresses within the city.

Vienna's Flak Towers were strategically located in four key areas: the Leitturm in Esterhazypark (Bezirk Mariahilf), the Gefechtsturm in Stiftskaserne (Bezirk Neubau), Arenbergpark, and Augarten. Each location was chosen to maximize defensive coverage of the city, creating overlapping fields of anti-aircraft fire. The towers' positions also highlighted their propaganda value, as they dominated the skyline and reminded citizens of the Nazi regime's power.

The Dark Side of Their Legacy

While the Flak Towers were designed as defensive measures, their very existence underscores the depths of the Nazi regime's exploitation and militarization of society. Thousands of forced laborers endured horrific conditions to construct these monoliths, often working without adequate food, medical care, or safety measures. Many died during construction, their suffering buried in the foundations of the towers.

Moreover, the towers symbolize the broader destruction wrought by the Nazi regime. Vienna, a city that had once been a beacon of culture and intellectualism, was co-opted into the machinery of war.

The Flak Tower in Augarten

The towers' presence in the cityscape represents the militarization of everyday life and the prioritization of warfare over the well-being of civilians.

Post-War Realities

After the war, the Flak Towers posed a significant dilemma for the Allied occupation forces and the Austrian government. Their immense size and reinforced concrete made them nearly impossible to demolish with the technology of the time. Attempts to destroy the towers often failed, and in some cases, the surrounding neighborhoods suffered more damage than the towers themselves.

Instead of removing these symbols of war, the Austrian authorities opted to repurpose some of them. The Leitturm in Esterhazypark (Bezirk Mariahilf) now houses the Haus des Meeres aquarium, while the Gefechtsturm in Stiftskaserne (Bezirk Neubau) became a military storage facility. The Flak Tower in Arenbergpark was left largely unused, and in Augarten, one of the towers now houses a museum, an attempt to integrate the structure into Vienna's modern identity. However, these efforts remain controversial, as many view the towers as enduring symbols of oppression and suffering.

Memory and Reflection

The Flak Towers' continued presence in Vienna raises important questions about how societies confront their dark histories. These structures, unmissable yet often overlooked, force residents and visitors alike to grapple with the legacy of war and totalitarianism. Should they be preserved as historical artifacts? Should they be repurposed for modern use? Or should they be erased entirely?

Some argue that the towers should serve as memorials, dedicated to the victims of Nazism and the countless lives lost during the war. Others believe that their imposing presence serves as a warning against the dangers of authoritarianism and militarism. Yet, there is also the risk of these structures becoming desensitized relics, their historical significance fading as they are absorbed into the urban fabric.

Augarten

Historical Significance: The Augarten is a public park and one of Vienna's oldest Baroque gardens, dating back to the early 18th century. It is renowned for its perfectly symmetrical layout, grand alleys, and cultural landmarks. The park is also home to two imposing Flak Towers, remnants of World War II, as well as the Augarten Porcelain Manufactory, where fine porcelain has been produced since 1718.

Address: Obere Augartenstraße 1, 1020 Vienna

Public transport: U2 to Taborstraße, Tram 31 to Obere Augartenstraße

Opening hours: Daily: 6 a.m. – 9 p.m. (March-October); 6 a.m. – 7 p.m. (November-February)

Arenbergpark

Historical Significance: Arenbergpark is a public park located in Vienna's 3rd district, Landstraße. Known for its serene atmosphere, it features wide green spaces, tree-lined paths, and two massive Flak

Towers that serve as striking reminders of Vienna's World War II history. Today, the park is a popular spot for relaxation and recreation.

Address: Neulinggasse, 1030 Vienna

Public transport: U3 to Rochusgasse, Tram O to Rasumofskygasse

Opening hours: Open 24 hours daily

Esterházypark

Historical Significance: Esterházypark is a public park located in Vienna's 6th district, Mariahilf. It is best known for housing one of Vienna's iconic Flak Towers, now repurposed as the Haus des Meeres aquarium and terrarium. This tower serves as a unique blend of historical monument and modern attraction, drawing visitors interested in both history and marine life.

Address: Fritz-Grünbaum-Platz 1, 1060 Vienna

Public transport: U3, U6 to Westbahnhof, Tram 6 or 18 to Gumpendorfer Straße

Opening hours: Park: Open 24 hours daily

Haus des Meeres: Mon-Sun: 9 a.m. – 6 p.m. (Thurs until 9 p.m.)

Online: https://www.haus-des-meeres.at/e

THE MUSEUM OF MILITARY HISTORY

The Museum of Military History (Heeresgeschichtliches Museum) in Vienna stands as one of the city's most significant and oldest museums, showcasing Austria's vast and complex military history. Located in the Arsenal, a historic military complex in Vienna's 3rd district, the museum is a treasure trove of artifacts, documents, and exhibitions that span centuries, from the early Habsburg empire to the end of World War II.

As a place that reflects the tumultuous military past of Austria, the Heeresgeschichtliches Museum offers a detailed examination of key events, figures, and battles that shaped not only the country but also the broader history of Europe. Through its extensive collection, visitors can explore the evolution of warfare, political changes, and the impact of military conflicts on society. In this essay, we will delve into the history of the museum, its architecture, and the significance of its collections, along with its place in the broader context of Austrian and European history.

History of the Museum

The Heeresgeschichtliches Museum was inaugurated in 1891, making it one of the oldest museums of its kind in the world. Its foundation is deeply intertwined with the legacy of the Habsburg Monarchy, which was, at the time, one of Europe's most powerful and expansive empires. The decision to establish a museum dedicated to military history came as a way to document and glorify the empire's military achievements, particularly during a period of increasing nationalism and imperial pride.

Museum of Military History

The museum's location, the Arsenal, was chosen for its historical significance. Built between 1848 and 1856 after the revolutionary uprisings of 1848, the Arsenal was initially intended to serve as a military barracks and armory. Its construction symbolized the reassertion of imperial power after the revolutions that had shaken much of Europe. The architecture of the Arsenal reflects the Habsburgs' desire to showcase both military might and artistic sophistication, with its red brick facades and neo-Byzantine, neo-Romanesque design.

Over the years, the museum's purpose evolved. What began as a place to commemorate Austria's military victories gradually became a repository of knowledge about all aspects of Austrian military history, including the tragedies of defeat and the horrors of war. After the dissolution of the Austro-Hungarian Empire following World War I, the museum adapted to the new realities of a smaller, independent Austrian republic. The museum's collections grew to include more modern conflicts, such as World War I and II, making it a comprehensive record of Austria's military past.

Architecture of the Heeresgeschichtliches Museum

The museum's architecture is an integral part of its identity. Designed by Theophil Hansen, a prominent Danish-Austrian architect, the museum building reflects a blend of various architectural styles. Hansen was known for his eclectic approach, drawing inspiration from the Byzantine, Moorish, and Renaissance traditions. The result is a structure that is both imposing and artistically refined, with richly decorated facades and grand interiors.

The main hall, or Feldherrenhalle (Hall of the Generals), is one of the museum's most striking features. This grand, vaulted space is adorned with statues of famous military figures from Austria's history, including Prince Eugene of Savoy and Archduke Charles. These statues, along with the numerous frescoes and murals depicting key battles, create an atmosphere of reverence and awe, underscoring the importance of Austria's military leaders in shaping the nation's destiny.

The Arsenal complex itself is vast, with numerous buildings that once housed armories, workshops, and barracks. Today, it serves as a fitting location for the Museum of Military History, given its origins as a military facility. The museum's exterior reflects the grandeur of the Habsburg era, with its red brick walls and turrets evoking the image of a fortress, while its interior is a testament to Austria's artistic heritage, with intricate woodwork, stained glass, and detailed sculptures.

Exhibitions and Collections

The Heeresgeschichtliches Museum is home to one of the largest and most comprehensive collections of military artifacts in Europe. Its exhibitions are divided chronologically, covering several key periods in Austrian military history. Each section of the museum offers insight into different conflicts, political developments, and technological advancements, providing a holistic view of Austria's role in European military affairs.

The Thirty Years' War and the Ottoman Wars

One of the museum's most fascinating sections covers the period of the Thirty Years' War (1618–1648) and Austria's conflicts with the Ottoman Empire. These wars were crucial in shaping the early Habsburg state and its defense of Central Europe against external threats. Visitors can view a variety of period weaponry, including muskets, swords, and armor, as well as paintings and maps that document these wars.

A highlight of this section is the Turkish Chamber, which contains numerous artifacts from the Ottoman sieges of Vienna in 1529 and 1683. The collection includes captured Turkish banners, weapons, and uniforms, offering a glimpse into the military culture of the Ottoman Empire and the significance of these conflicts in European history.

The Napoleonic Wars and the Congress of Vienna

The museum also contains a large collection dedicated to the Napoleonic Wars, during which Austria played a pivotal role in the struggle against Napoleon Bonaparte's expanding empire. The Napoleonic section features uniforms, weapons, and other artifacts from the era, as well as models and dioramas depicting key battles, such as the Battle of Austerlitz in 1805.

One of the most important figures represented in this section is Archduke Charles, who was instrumental in Austria's military efforts against Napoleon. His portrait, along with a detailed account of his campaigns, highlights his role as a national hero and military strategist.

World War I and the Assassination of Archduke Franz Ferdinand

A significant portion of the museum is dedicated to World War I, one of the most devastating conflicts in human history and a key turning point for Austria. The museum's World War I collection is particularly notable for its detailed coverage of the assassination of Archduke Franz Ferdinand, an event that sparked the war. The car in which Franz Ferdinand and his wife, Sophie, Duchess of Hohenberg, were assassinated in Sarajevo in 1914 is one of the museum's most famous exhibits.

In addition to the car, visitors can see the archduke's bloodstained uniform and the pistol used by his assassin, Gavrilo Princip. These artifacts bring to life the events that led to the outbreak of World War I and provide a personal connection to one of the most significant moments in 20th-century history.

The museum's World War I section also includes weapons, uniforms, and other military equipment used by Austrian and German soldiers during the war. Maps, photographs, and personal letters further illustrate the scale and human cost of the conflict.

World War II and the Aftermath

The Heeresgeschichtliches Museum also delves into the dark period of World War II and Austria's role in the conflict. This section covers the Anschluss (the annexation of Austria by Nazi Germany in 1938) and the subsequent participation of Austrian soldiers in the war. The museum examines the impact of the war on Austria and the atrocities committed during the Holocaust, reflecting the complex legacy of this period in the country's history.

Artifacts in this section include weapons, vehicles, and military equipment from both the Axis and Allied powers, as well as personal belongings of soldiers and civilians. The museum's approach to this period is both sobering and educational, encouraging reflection on the horrors of war and the importance of remembrance.

Conclusion: A Monument to Austria's Military Heritage

The Heeresgeschichtliches Museum stands as a testament to Austria's long and complex military history. From the early Habsburg wars against the Ottoman Empire to the global conflicts of the 20th century, the museum provides a comprehensive look at the evolution of warfare and its impact on Austrian society. Its vast collection of artifacts, combined with its striking architecture and historical significance, make it a must-visit destination for anyone interested in history, politics, or military strategy.

In a city known for its rich cultural heritage, the Heeresgeschichtliches Museum offers a unique perspective on the role of the military in shaping Vienna's past and present.

Heeresgeschichtliches Museum | Museum of Military History

Historical Significance: The Heeresgeschichtliches Museum is Austria's premier institution dedicated to military history. It houses artifacts and exhibits that span centuries, covering the Ottoman Wars, the Napoleonic Wars, the Austro-Hungarian Empire, and both World Wars. Notable exhibits include the car in which Archduke Franz Ferdinand was assassinated, an event that triggered World War I. The museum is located in the historic Arsenal complex, offering an insightful look into Austria's military past.

Address: Arsenal, Objekt 1, 1030 Vienna

Public transport: Tram D to Heeresgeschichtliches Museum

Opening hours: Daily: 9 a.m. – 5 p.m.; Closed on Mondays Online: www.hgm.at

THE TWO SIEGES BY THE OTTOMAN ARMY

Vienna, the heart of Europe, with its imperial palaces, glittering ballrooms, and grand cathedrals, is often remembered for its glorious music, arts, and imperial history. However, hidden in the city's cobblestone streets and ancient fortifications lies a darker chapter—Vienna's two sieges by the Ottoman Empire, moments when the fate of Europe hung in the balance.

The First Siege of Vienna (1529)

The first Ottoman siege of Vienna occurred in 1529 under the reign of Sultan Suleiman the Magnificent, the most powerful ruler of the Ottoman Empire. Suleiman's empire stretched from the Balkans to the Middle East, and after his conquest of Hungary in 1526 at the Battle of Mohács, Vienna became the next target in his expansionist vision.

Prelude to the Siege

The strategic importance of Vienna was immense. It stood as the gateway to Western Europe and was considered the last bastion of Christianity against the advancing forces of Islam. Suleiman, with an army of nearly 120,000 men, set out to capture the city in what he hoped would be the culmination of his European campaign.

According to tradition, a journeyman baker, through his alertness, discovered the Ottomans who had dug deep beneath the city using mines in 1529, enabling their timely repulsion. Address: Heidenschuß 3, 1010 Vienna Public transport: U3 to Herrengasse; Tram 1, 71, D to Stephansplatz

However, Suleiman's march to Vienna was fraught with difficulties. His army was hampered by heavy rains that turned the roads into rivers of mud, slowing the advance. Additionally, Vienna's defenders, under the leadership of Austrian military commander Count Niklas Salm, had prepared the city's defenses, despite their small garrison of around 15,000 men.

The Siege

On September 27, 1529, Suleiman's forces arrived at the gates of Vienna. The Ottoman army, renowned for its discipline and engineering prowess, began to dig trenches and set up cannons to bombard the city walls. Suleiman hoped to breach the city's fortifications and quickly overwhelm the defenders.

However, the Ottomans met fierce resistance. The defenders, knowing they were heavily outnumbered, put up an extraordinary fight. The citizens of Vienna, including women and children, took part in the defense, helping to repair the walls and dig counter-trenches. The Ottomans launched several frontal assaults on the city but were repelled each time.

As the siege wore on, the situation inside the city grew desperate, with food and supplies running low. Yet, winter was approaching, and the Ottomans, unprepared for a long siege, found their supply lines stretched and morale faltering. The weather turned against the invaders, with heavy rains and the onset of frost making life in the Ottoman camp unbearable.

Withdrawal

On October 14, 1529, after weeks of unsuccessful assaults and deteriorating conditions, Suleiman ordered his army to withdraw. The first siege of Vienna had ended in failure, and the Ottoman forces retreated back to the Balkans. Vienna had held, and with it, the heart of Europe was saved—for the time being.

Although the siege had failed, it marked a turning point in European history. The Ottoman Empire remained a formidable threat, but Vienna's defense was hailed as a victory for Christian Europe. The Habsburgs, who ruled Austria, emerged as defenders of Christendom, a reputation that would shape their future policies and alliances.

The Second Siege of Vienna (1683)

Nearly 150 years after Suleiman's failed attempt, Vienna would once again find itself under siege by the Ottoman forces. This time, the attack came under Sultan Mehmed IV, and the stakes were even higher. The Ottoman Empire, though still powerful, was beginning to show signs of decline. The siege of Vienna in 1683 was an attempt to reassert Ottoman dominance over Europe.

Prelude to the Siege

The Ottoman Empire, led by Grand Vizier Kara Mustafa Pasha, had once again set its sights on Vienna. This time, the Ottomans were not merely interested in conquest; they saw Vienna as a stepping stone to further expansion into Europe. Kara Mustafa, an ambitious and ruthless leader, had dreams of marching into Paris and Rome after taking Vienna.

In the summer of 1683, Kara Mustafa gathered an army of nearly 150,000 men and began his march toward Vienna. The city, under the rule of Emperor Leopold I of the Habsburg dynasty, was ill-prepared for the coming onslaught. Leopold and much of the Austrian nobility fled the city, leaving its defense to Count Ernst Rüdiger von Starhemberg and a garrison of around 15,000 soldiers.

After the victory against the Turks at the Battle of Kahlenberg (September 12, 1683), Leopold had the chapel rebuilt and in 1693 dedicated it to Saint Leopold, after which the mountain was named Leopoldsberg.

The Siege

On July 14, 1683, the Ottoman army surrounded Vienna. The situation was dire. Vienna's defenses, though solid, were no match for the massive Ottoman artillery. The city's food supplies quickly dwindled, and disease began to spread among the defenders. But unlike the first siege, Vienna was not alone.

A heavy stone is believed to have been fired from a mortar by the Ottomans from Leopoldstadt during the siege of Vienna. Address: Sterngasse 3, 1010 Vienna Public transport: U1, U3 to Stephansplatz; Tram 1, 71, D to Rathausplatz/Burgtheater

The Holy Roman Empire and the Polish-Lithuanian Commonwealth had formed an alliance to counter the Ottoman threat. The leader of this Christian coalition was King Jan III Sobieski of Poland, a military genius who would play a crucial role in the defense of Vienna.

As the siege dragged on, Kara Mustafa grew impatient. He launched repeated assaults on the city, but each time, the defenders managed to hold the line. The Ottomans dug tunnels under the city walls, hoping to detonate explosives and cause a breach. But the Viennese defenders, using counter-tunneling techniques, thwarted many of these attempts.

The Relief of Vienna

As September approached, the situation inside Vienna grew desperate. The Ottomans were on the verge of breaking through the city's defenses. But help was on the way. On September 6, 1683, King Jan III Sobieski arrived with a relief army of around 70,000 men, composed of Polish, German, and Austrian forces.

On September 12, 1683, the decisive Battle of Vienna took place. Sobieski, leading the largest cavalry charge in history with his famed Polish Winged Hussars, smashed through the Ottoman lines. The Ottomans, caught off guard by the sudden arrival of the relief force, were thrown into disarray. Kara Mustafa's army was routed, and the Ottomans fled the battlefield in panic.

Aftermath

The second siege of Vienna was over. The defeat at Vienna marked the beginning of the end for Ottoman expansion into Europe. Over the next few decades, the Ottomans would be driven back from much of their European territories, and the Habsburgs, along with their allies, would consolidate their power in the region.

Kara Mustafa, humiliated by the defeat, was executed on the orders of Sultan Mehmed IV. His failure to capture Vienna had sealed his fate, and the Ottoman Empire would never again pose the same threat to Europe.

For Vienna, the victory was a turning point. The city's survival during the second siege solidified its role as a bulwark of Western Europe. It became a symbol of resistance against the encroaching forces of the Ottoman Empire and a testament to the resilience of its defenders.

The Dark Legacy of the Sieges

The two sieges of Vienna were not just military confrontations; they were cultural and religious clashes that shaped the history of Europe. The Ottoman Empire, representing the Islamic world, had twice attempted to conquer Vienna, the heart of Christian Europe. Both times, the city had survived, and with it, the balance of power in Europe was maintained.

But the legacy of these sieges left a darker mark on Vienna. The fear of Ottoman invasion haunted the city for centuries, influencing its architecture, its art, and its politics. The walls of Vienna, rebuilt and reinforced after each siege, stood as a reminder of the city's precarious position on the frontier between East and West.

The Cossack Monument in the Türkenschanzpark, where Ottoman trenches were located during the 1683 siege, honors the contribution of the Ukrainian Cossack army in the relief battle on September 12, 1683. Address: Türkenschanzpark, 1180 Vienna Public transport: Tram 40, 41 to Aumannplatz; Bus 40A to Türkenschanzplatz

The dark side of Vienna's history, marked by the bloodshed and destruction of the Ottoman sieges, is an essential part of understanding the city's complex past.

Stephansdom | St. Stephen's Cathedral

Historical Significance: St. Stephen's Cathedral holds significant historical ties to the Ottoman sieges of Vienna. The famous Pummerin bell, housed in the cathedral, was cast from melted-down Ottoman cannonballs left behind after the second siege in 1683.

Address: Stephansplatz 3, 1010 Vienna

Public transport: U1, U3 to Stephansplatz

Opening hours: Daily: 6 a.m. – 10 p.m.

Online: www.stephansdom.at

Augarten

Historical Significance: Augarten was part of the battlefield during the second Ottoman siege of 1683. The Ottoman forces dug trenches in this area as they attempted to breach Vienna's defenses. Address: Obere Augartenstraße 1, 1020 Vienna

Public transport: U2 to Taborstraße; Tram 31 to Obere Augartenstraße

Opening hours: Daily: 6 a.m. – 9 p.m.

Online: www.augarten.at

Belvedere

Historical Significance: The Belvedere palace was the residence of Prince Eugene of Savoy, the military commander who defeated the Ottoman forces. His leadership was a turning point in the war against the Ottoman Empire.

Address: Prinz Eugen-Straße 27, 1030 Vienna

Public transport: Tram D to Schloss Belvedere

Opening hours: Daily: 10 a.m. – 6 p.m.

Online: www.belvedere.at

Karlskirche | St. Charles Church

Historical Significance: Karlskirche was commissioned by Emperor Charles VI after the successful defense of Vienna from the Ottoman siege in 1683. The church is a tribute to Saint Charles Borromeo, whom the emperor had prayed to for protection. It stands as a reminder of Vienna's victory over the Ottomans.

Address: Karlsplatz, 1040 Vienna

Public transport: U1, U2, U4 to Karlsplatz

Opening hours: Daily: 9 a.m. – 6 p.m.

Online: www.karlskirche.at

ELISABETH BÁTHORY: THE BLOOD COUNTESS

Countess Elisabeth Báthory, often referred to as the "Blood Countess," is one of the most infamous figures in European history. Born in 1560 into one of the most powerful noble families of Hungary, Báthory's legacy has been marred by legends of unspeakable cruelty. She is often depicted as a woman obsessed with maintaining her youth by bathing in the blood of young girls, a dark tale that has cemented her place in history as one of the most prolific female serial killers.

With over 650 alleged victims, her crimes are believed to have spanned several decades before she was arrested in 1610. However, much of Báthory's life, including her ties to Vienna and her social connections, reveals a much more nuanced, if still deeply unsettling, picture.

Elisabeth Báthory's Origins and Political Power

Elisabeth Báthory was born into a family of immense wealth and influence. The Báthorys were one of the most prominent noble families in Central Europe, with connections extending across Hungary, Poland, and Transylvania. Elisabeth's uncle, Stephen Báthory, was the

King of Poland and the Grand Duke of Lithuania, while her family's influence stretched across the Hungarian nobility.

Despite her later infamy, Elisabeth grew up in the privileged environment of Hungarian aristocracy, receiving an education that was rare for women of her time. She spoke several languages, including Hungarian, Latin, and German, and was known to be highly intelligent. In 1575, she married Ferenc Nádasdy, another powerful Hungarian nobleman, further cementing her position within the upper echelons of Central European society. Nádasdy was often away at war, leaving Báthory in control of their vast estates, which included Čachtice Castle, where most of her alleged crimes would later take place.

Augustinerstraße

Connections to the Habsburg Court

Though much of Báthory's infamous legacy is tied to her estates in Hungary and Slovakia, her ties to Vienna and the Habsburg court cannot be overlooked. Vienna, at the time, was a hub of political intrigue and cultural importance.

As the capital of the Habsburg Monarchy, the city played a central role in the politics of the region, and for a figure like Báthory—whose family wielded enormous power—it was a significant location.

Vienna was home to numerous Hungarian nobles, many of whom, like Báthory, maintained close ties to the Habsburg court. The Holy Roman Emperor Rudolf II, who reigned from 1576 to 1612, ruled from Prague, but Vienna remained a critical center of political and diplomatic affairs. As part of the Hungarian aristocracy, Báthory and her husband would have had frequent interactions with the Habsburg court, whether through official duties or social engagements. Vienna, with its palatial architecture and imperial splendor, was a city where Báthory would have moved in elite circles.

Augustinerstraße 12

While in Vienna, Báthory stayed in a residence on Augustinerstraße 12, near Albertinaplatz and the famous Vienna Opera. This historic building, with its Baroque facade, still stands today as a reminder of the city's grand architectural heritage. Though it is not open to the public, visitors can admire the building from the outside, appreciating the mysterious aura that seems to linger in its walls, a faint echo of the blood-soaked legend that continues to shadow the Countess's name. The residence transports you back to Vienna's Baroque era, a time inextricably linked with figures like Báthory, whose lives played out amidst the political and social complexities of their time.

Addresses in Vienna: Nobility and Power

At the height of her influence, it is likely that Báthory stayed in some of the most exclusive areas of Vienna, which were home to the city's nobility. Though her primary residences were Čachtice Castle and her estate in Sárvár, Vienna was a crucial city for any noble with aspirations of power and influence in the Habsburg territories.

Vienna's Innere Stadt (First District), with its grand palaces and proximity to the Hofburg, would have been a logical place for someone of Báthory's status to stay. The aristocratic families of Hungary, many of whom had close ties to the Habsburg court, often maintained homes in this central part of the city. Nobles who visited the capital would frequently stay in grand townhouses or palaces, such as those located near Stephansplatz or along the Graben, one of Vienna's most famous streets.

Given her aristocratic status, it is also plausible that Báthory had dealings with prominent Viennese families. Many Hungarian nobles who visited Vienna interacted with the powerful Khevenhüller, Esterházy, and Pálffy families, among others, who were influential figures in the Habsburg court. These families had substantial political and military influence, and it is possible that Báthory engaged with them in matters related to her estates and wealth.

Whether she fully confessed to the priest at Augustinerkirche or not, we will never know.

Vienna's Role in the Fall of Báthory

Vienna also played a significant role in Báthory's eventual downfall. By the early 1600s, rumors of her cruelty began to spread. It was said that young girls from nearby villages were brought to her castle, never to return. According to testimony gathered during the investigations, Báthory and her accomplices were responsible for torturing and murdering hundreds of young women. Though much of the evidence was based on hearsay, the accusations were severe enough to prompt an investigation by King Matthias II of Hungary, a member of the Habsburg family.

Matthias II, who ruled as the Holy Roman Emperor from 1612 to 1619, was deeply connected to Vienna and oversaw the investigation into Báthory's alleged crimes. The trial, which took place in 1611, was not held in Vienna but in Bytča, Slovakia, near Báthory's Čachtice Castle. However, Matthias II's court was based in Vienna, and it was from there that the imperial orders for the investigation and subsequent punishment of Báthory were issued.

Although Báthory was never formally tried or sentenced, her punishment was swift and brutal. She was placed under house arrest in Čachtice Castle, where she lived in isolation until her death in 1614. It is worth noting that the political motivations behind her arrest were likely influenced by her vast wealth and power. The Habsburgs, always wary of overly powerful nobles, may have seen her downfall as an opportunity to seize her lands and diminish the influence of the Hungarian aristocracy.

Legacy and the Myth of the Blood Countess

Elisabeth Báthory's legacy is one that blends historical fact with legend. While it is undeniable that she was involved in the deaths of numerous young women, the extent of her guilt remains debated. Some historians argue that the charges against her were exaggerated, perhaps even fabricated, to discredit her and seize her lands. Others believe that she was a true psychopath, driven by a desire for eternal youth—a desire she sought to fulfill through ritualistic murder.

Her connections to Vienna, however, remain a fascinating aspect of her life. The city was not just a place of political intrigue and power but also a backdrop to the machinations of a woman whose name would become synonymous with cruelty. Vienna's aristocratic circles, particularly the Habsburg court, provided the context for her rise to power, and later, her downfall.

A Tale of Power, Blood, and Intrigue

Elisabeth Báthory's connections to Vienna reveal the city as an integral part of her life, not just as a political center but also as a place where the intrigues of the nobility played out. Her stays in the city would have brought her into contact with the most powerful figures of the time. Vienna's grand streets and noble palaces were a fitting stage for a woman whose life would end in infamy, and whose legacy as the "Blood Countess" would continue to captivate and horrify generations.

In the end, Vienna was a city that both shaped and witnessed the rise and fall of one of history's most enigmatic figures. The story of Elisabeth Báthory continues to linger in the dark corridors of history, a reminder of the perils of unchecked power and the terrifying depths of human cruelty.

VIENNA'S KRIMINALMUSEUM

The Kriminalmuseum in Vienna offers a fascinating and chilling glimpse into the city's criminal past. Located in the historic district of Leopoldstadt, the museum is dedicated to chronicling the history of crime, law enforcement, and justice in Vienna and Austria more broadly. Housed in an old building that adds to the atmosphere of its exhibitions, the museum covers a wide range of criminal activity, from medieval punishments to modern forensic science, making it one of Vienna's most unique and engaging museums.

Through an extensive collection of exhibits, including weapons, forensic evidence, photographs, and historical documents, the Kriminalmuseum presents a journey through Austria's darker history. It reveals the evolving nature of crime and punishment, the development of legal systems, and the ways in which societies have sought to deal with criminal behavior. In this essay, we will explore the history of the museum, its significance, and the highlights of its collection, shedding light on a side of Vienna that is often overlooked.

The History and Significance of the Kriminalmuseum

The Kriminalmuseum is located in one of Vienna's oldest districts, in a building that itself holds historical significance. Originally part of a medieval hospital, the museum's location adds to its macabre allure. The building's old stone walls, narrow corridors, and dim lighting help to create an eerie, immersive experience, making visitors feel as though they are stepping back in time to witness the darker aspects of Vienna's history.

Vienna Crime Museum (Wiener Kriminalmuseum)

Founded in the 19th century, the museum began as a collection of items related to crime, punishment, and forensic science. Over time, the museum's collection grew as it incorporated more artifacts and materials, evolving into the comprehensive institution it is today. The Kriminalmuseum now serves not only as a window into Vienna's criminal history but also as a reflection of societal attitudes towards crime and justice over the centuries.

The museum's exhibits are organized chronologically, beginning with medieval times and continuing up to the modern era. This arrangement allows visitors to trace the evolution of crime and punishment in Vienna, from the harsh and brutal justice of the Middle

Ages to the more sophisticated and scientific methods of the 20th century. Along the way, the museum provides valuable insights into the nature of crime, the legal system, and the role of law enforcement in maintaining order.

Medieval Crime and Punishment

The **Kriminalmuseum** begins its story with a focus on medieval crime and punishment, a period when justice was often swift and brutal. The exhibits from this era showcase the tools of torture and execution that were used to punish criminals and maintain public order. Among the most striking items on display are the instruments of medieval justice, including executioner's axes, branding irons, and devices used for public humiliation, such as stocks and pillories.

During the Middle Ages, punishments were designed not only to punish the criminal but also to serve as a deterrent to others. Public executions, for example, were common in Vienna, and criminals were often hanged or beheaded in front of large crowds. The museum vividly portrays this aspect of Vienna's past through historical illustrations, woodcuts, and relics of these grim events. The use of torture as a means of extracting confessions was also widespread, and the museum contains several instruments used for this purpose, including the infamous rack and thumbscrews.

One of the most interesting aspects of the medieval section of the museum is its exploration of how justice was dispensed by different authorities. During this period, local lords and magistrates had significant control over the administration of justice, and punishment could vary widely depending on the region and the individual in charge. The museum illustrates this decentralized approach to justice through court records and documents from the period, providing a glimpse into the often arbitrary nature of medieval law.

The Criminal Underworld of the 18th and 19th Centuries

As the Kriminalmuseum moves into the 18th and 19th centuries, the exhibits focus on the rise of organized crime and the development of a more formalized system of law enforcement. During this time, Vienna was growing rapidly, and with urbanization came new challenges for maintaining law and order. The city's burgeoning population created opportunities for thieves, pickpockets, and con artists to thrive, and the museum details many of the most notorious criminal cases from this era.

One of the highlights of this section is the exploration of the Viennese underworld, which included notorious gangs and criminal organizations that operated throughout the city. Through photographs, police reports, and personal accounts, the museum paints a vivid picture of the criminal activity that flourished in Vienna's streets and alleys. Visitors can learn about infamous criminals such as Johann Georg Grasel, a notorious bandit who became a folk legend in Austria for his daring exploits. Grasel's story, along with others, is brought to life through the display of personal items, such as weapons and clothing, used by the criminals of the time.

The 19th century also saw significant advancements in the field of forensic science, and the museum features an extensive collection of tools and techniques used by early detectives and criminologists to solve crimes. One particularly intriguing exhibit focuses on the development of criminal profiling and forensic pathology, showing how these emerging sciences helped law enforcement track down criminals more effectively. Items on display include early forensic tools, fingerprinting kits, and photographs from crime scenes, illustrating the growing sophistication of police work during this period.

Infamous Criminal Cases

Throughout its exhibits, the Kriminalmuseum highlights some of the most infamous criminal cases in Vienna's history. These cases often captured the public's imagination and continue to be remembered as part of the city's dark folklore. One of the most notorious cases is that of Elisabeth Báthory, the so-called "Blood Countess," who is said to have murdered hundreds of young women in the early 17th century. Though she lived in Hungary, her trial and imprisonment had a profound impact on the region, and the museum explores her life and crimes in detail.

Another infamous case is that of Hugo Schenk, a serial killer active in Vienna in the late 19th century. Schenk, known as the "Ladies' Killer," was responsible for the deaths of several women whom he lured with promises of marriage. His gruesome crimes shocked Vienna and led to his execution in 1884. The museum presents the story of his arrest and trial, complete with original court documents and newspaper clippings from the time.

The Kriminalmuseum also covers the story of Franz Fuchs, one of Austria's most notorious modern criminals. Fuchs was a far-right extremist responsible for a series of letter bomb attacks in the 1990s that targeted immigrants and human rights activists. His arrest and subsequent trial are documented through police reports, photographs, and media coverage, offering visitors a chilling glimpse into the mind of a modern terrorist.

The Rise of Modern Policing and Forensics

As the museum progresses into the 20th century, it shifts focus to the development of modern policing and forensic science. The early 20th century was a time of rapid innovation in law enforcement, and the museum showcases many of the technological advancements that helped police solve crimes more efficiently. Visitors can explore early versions of lie detectors, ballistic analysis tools, and the first police databases, which revolutionized the way criminals were tracked and apprehended.

One of the key figures in this transformation was Hans Gross, an Austrian criminologist and the founder of modern forensic science. Gross's contributions to the field are well documented in the museum, with several exhibits dedicated to his pioneering work in criminal investigation. His book, Criminal Investigation, is considered one of the foundational texts of forensic science, and the museum displays original copies of this work along with personal items belonging to Gross.

The museum also explores the role of fingerprinting, which became a standard tool in law enforcement during the early 20th century. Through interactive displays, visitors can learn how fingerprints were first used to solve crimes and see examples of early fingerprint analysis. Additionally, the museum covers the history of ballistics, showing how firearms were analyzed to match bullets to specific weapons, a technique that remains crucial in modern criminal investigations.

Crime and Society

Beyond simply documenting criminal acts, the Kriminalmuseum also examines the broader social context in which these crimes occurred. The museum explores how economic conditions, political unrest, and social inequality have contributed to rising crime rates throughout Vienna's history. For example, the museum delves into the impact of poverty and unemployment during the 19th century, which led to an increase in theft, burglary, and other petty crimes.

The role of women in crime is another important theme addressed by the museum. Throughout history, women have been both victims and perpetrators of crime, and the Kriminalmuseum sheds light on some of the most notable female criminals in Vienna's history.

From notorious poisoners to daring thieves, these women often defied societal expectations and used their cunning to commit crimes that shocked the public.

The museum also addresses the changing nature of punishment over the centuries. In earlier periods, public executions and corporal punishment were common, but by the 20th century, the focus had shifted towards rehabilitation and imprisonment. The museum traces this evolution through exhibits on Vienna's early prisons and penal institutions, showing how attitudes towards crime and punishment have shifted over time.

The Kriminalmuseum in Vienna provides a unique and compelling look at the city's criminal history. Through its extensive collection of artifacts, documents, and exhibits, the museum offers visitors an opportunity to explore the darker side of Vienna's past while also gaining insights into the evolution of crime, punishment, and law enforcement.

By showcasing both infamous criminals and the development of forensic science, the museum highlights how society has grappled with the challenge of maintaining law and order over the centuries. It is a place where visitors can reflect on the complexities of justice, the causes of crime, and the enduring fascination with criminal behavior. Whether you are interested in history, law, or simply the macabre, the Kriminalmuseum offers an unforgettable journey into Vienna's criminal underworld.

Wiener Kriminalmuseum | Vienna Crime Museum

Historical Significance: The Wiener Kriminalmuseum offers a fascinating and sometimes chilling look into Vienna's history of crime and law enforcement. The museum's exhibits cover centuries of criminal cases, forensic science, and the justice system, including some of Austria's most notorious crimes and criminals. Housed in a historic building, the museum provides a unique perspective on the darker side of Vienna's past.

Address: Große Sperlgasse 24, 1020 Vienna

Public transport: U2 to Taborstraße; Tram 2 to Taborstraße Opening hours: Daily: 10 a.m. – 5 p.m.; Closed on Mondays

Online: www.kriminalmuseum.at

THE FUNERAL MUSEUM

Vienna has long been associated with a particular reverence for death, with elaborate funerary practices dating back centuries. As the capital of the Habsburg Empire, the city became a focal point for grandiose and solemn burial rites, especially within the aristocratic and royal circles. The influence of the Catholic Church in shaping these customs was profound, from the pomp and ceremony of state funerals to the humble, yet no less significant, burial traditions of the working classes.

Vienna's Central Cemetery (Zentralfriedhof), established in 1874, is one of the largest cemeteries in Europe and the final resting place for over three million people. It houses not only the graves of common citizens but also an impressive collection of tombs dedicated to famous figures such as Ludwig van Beethoven, Johann Strauss, and Franz Schubert. The funeral culture in Vienna evolved alongside the city's growth, with increasingly sophisticated burial services and customs being established over the centuries.

Funeral Attire and Mourning Clothes

It was within this context that the idea of a Funeral Museum emerged. Founded in 1967, the museum was originally housed in the city's central mortuary. However, it later moved to the Zentralfriedhof, where it could be more accessible to those visiting the cemetery. It became a way for people to understand the complex rituals and the significance that Viennese society places on death and remembrance.

The Exhibits: Exploring Vienna's Unique Funerary Traditions

The Funeral Museum presents a broad range of objects and exhibits that reveal Vienna's obsession with death and funerals. It holds over 1,000 exhibits, showcasing artifacts from the 18th century up to modern times. The museum walks visitors through the history of Viennese funeral customs, revealing how societal attitudes towards death have evolved.

Coffins and Caskets One of the most intriguing sections of the museum is the display of historical coffins and caskets. These range from simple wooden coffins used by the poorer classes to the opulent caskets of the wealthy. Notably, there is a fascinating exhibit on "reusable coffins," which were a peculiar innovation introduced during the reign of Emperor Joseph II in the late 18th century. Due to the overcrowding of cemeteries, Joseph II introduced coffins that had trapdoors to drop the deceased into the ground while the coffin itself was reused. However, this unpopular practice was quickly abandoned due to public outrage.

Death Masks and Post-Mortem Photography: The museum also features an array of death masks and post-mortem photographs, which were popular in Vienna during the 19th century. These served as mementos, allowing families to preserve the faces of their loved ones after death. Death masks were particularly significant during the 19th century, often being taken of famous personalities such as composers and political figures.

Funeral Attire and Mourning Clothes: Mourning attire is another fascinating exhibit in the museum. It provides insight into the strict social codes regarding how long a person was expected to mourn the death of a relative or spouse. Mourning clothes, especially for widows, were highly ritualized, with specific fabrics and colors (often black) being required for extended periods. The fashion of mourning also influenced daily life, affecting how people interacted with each other and observed social hierarchies.

Funeral Carriages and Hearses: The museum showcases funeral carriages, highlighting the importance of funeral processions in Viennese culture. These carriages, often ornately decorated, were used to transport the deceased to their final resting place in style. Some of the most luxurious carriages were reserved for the nobility and reflected the deceased's social status even in death. The grand funerary processions were a public spectacle and a way for the aristocracy to display their wealth and influence one last time.

Coffins and Caskets

The Role of the Gravedigger: An interesting aspect of the Funeral Museum is its attention to the role of the gravedigger, or "Totengräber," in Viennese society. The gravedigger has a special place in Viennese folklore, often portrayed as a somewhat macabre, yet necessary figure in maintaining the cemeteries. The museum highlights how these workers were integral to the functioning of burial services, often living within the cemeteries and being responsible for the physical act of burying the dead.

Funeral Music: Vienna, as the city of music, also brings its love of classical composition into its funeral traditions. The museum dedicates a section to the role of funeral music, featuring compositions specifically written for funeral services. It was common for musicians and composers to be hired to perform at the funerals of the wealthy. Special requiems were composed to honor the dead, and even today, music plays an essential part in Viennese funerals.

The Cult of Death in Vienna

Vienna's obsession with death is not simply about burial rituals, but rather reflects a cultural phenomenon known as the "Viennese cult of death." This culture has its roots in the Baroque period, when the Catholic Church's emphasis on the afterlife and the transitory nature of life on earth dominated religious and social thought. The elaborate rituals surrounding death—processions, masses, and even memento mori art—were not merely about honoring the deceased but about reminding the living of their own mortality.

The Funeral Museum encapsulates this "cult of death" by showing how death, while feared, was also revered as a fundamental part of life. In Vienna, death was often romanticized, and the ritual surrounding it was steeped in both dignity and drama. The museum helps visitors understand how the Viennese have always maintained a deep connection to death as an inevitable and significant part of life, a reflection of the broader existential questions of mortality.

The Role of the Undertaker (Bestattungswesen)

The Funeral Museum also shines a light on the role of the undertaker in Vienna. Known as the "Bestatter," the undertaker has long held an important role in organizing the final farewell of the deceased. Vienna's municipal funeral services (Bestattung Wien), which originated in the early 20th century, were among the most well-organized and elaborate in Europe. Bestattungs Wien became a symbol of efficiency and respect, providing services that catered to all classes, from simple burials to grand state funerals.

Exhibits in the museum display the various tools and techniques used by undertakers, such as embalming methods and the evolution of funeral technology. It also touches upon how funerals were conducted during wartime, as well as during the devastating Spanish flu pandemic.

Modern Funerary Practices

The museum not only looks to the past but also addresses modern funerary practices in Vienna. With changing social attitudes towards death, more and more people are choosing cremation, eco-friendly burials, or personalizing their funerals with non-religious ceremonies. The museum's exhibits highlight these trends and reflect how Vienna continues to adapt its funeral customs to the times while retaining its deep-seated respect for the dead.

Visiting the Funeral Museum

For visitors interested in the macabre, the Bestattungsmuseum offers a compelling look into Vienna's unique relationship with death. It stands as a testament to the city's enduring fascination with mortality and offers a thoughtful exploration of how funerals have shaped, and continue to shape, Vienna's cultural identity. Situated within the expansive Zentralfriedhof, a visit to the museum is not only an educational experience but also an opportunity to reflect on the role of death in shaping human history and culture.

As you wander through the Zentralfriedhof, where history, culture, and death converge, the Funeral Museum provides the perfect lens through which to understand Vienna's enduring and often elaborate relationship with the dead.

Bestattungsmuseum | Funeral Museum

Historical Significance: The Bestattungsmuseum explores the fascinating history of funeral customs and death in Vienna, a city known for its unique relationship with mortality. The museum features exhibits on burial traditions, mourning culture, and the famous Vienna Central Cemetery. Visitors can learn about the city's historical funeral rites, hearse carriages, and even view the famous "Viennese Coffin" designed to be reusable during the 18th century.

Address: Simmeringer Hauptstraße 234, 1110 Vienna (Vienna Central Cemetery)

Public transport: U3 to Simmering; Tram 6, 71 to Zentralfriedhof

Opening hours: Monday to Friday: 9 a.m. – 4:30 p.m.

Online: www.bestattungsmuseum.at

THE ZENTRALFRIEDHOF: VIENNA'S CITY OF THE DEAD

The Zentralfriedhof (Central Cemetery) in Vienna, Austria, is one of the largest cemeteries in the world and perhaps one of the most culturally significant. Sprawling over an area of about 620 acres, the cemetery is more than just a burial ground; it is a place that reflects the rich history, cultural diversity, and architectural grandeur of Vienna.

Opened in 1874, the Zentralfriedhof is a historical landmark, a tourist destination, and a place of pilgrimage for those wishing to pay their respects to many of the most famous figures in Austrian history. This essay will delve into the origins, architecture, notable residents, and cultural significance of the Zentralfriedhof, emphasizing its role as a mirror of Viennese society through the centuries.

A Brief History of the Zentralfriedhof

By the 19th century, Vienna was rapidly expanding, and with its growth came an increasing demand for burial space.

The Jewish section of the cemetery.

The city's existing cemeteries were becoming overcrowded, and it was clear that a new, larger burial site was needed to accommodate the city's growing population.

The decision to establish a central cemetery far beyond the city's periphery was part of an effort to create a more organized and efficient burial system.

In 1863, Vienna's city council commissioned the construction of the Zentralfriedhof, selecting a location far from the center in Simmering, a district southeast of the city. Though some critics at the time protested the choice of location as too remote, the cemetery's planners envisioned a vast necropolis capable of serving the city for centuries. The Zentralfriedhof officially opened on All Saints' Day, November 1, 1874, though its initial reception was less than warm, as it coincided with an outbreak of cholera in Vienna.

The cemetery was designed to be multi-denominational, making it unique in Europe at the time. This inclusivity reflected the Habsburg Empire's policy of religious tolerance, and even today, the Zentralfriedhof contains sections dedicated to Roman Catholics, Protestants, Jews, Muslims, Russian Orthodox, and many other religious groups.

The Buddhist section of the cemetery.

The cemetery's creation marked a major shift in the way Vienna, and by extension Europe, viewed death and burial, moving away from smaller, crowded cemeteries and toward a monumental, park-like environment that invited reflection, mourning, and even tourism.

The Architecture and Layout of the Cemetery

Designed in the manner of a grand park or garden, the Zentralfriedhof is not only a burial ground but a place of peaceful contemplation. Its extensive avenues are lined with trees, while grand monuments and ornate tombs blend seamlessly with more modest burial plots.

The cemetery's park-like atmosphere is designed to evoke a sense of timelessness and transcendence, allowing visitors to connect with nature and reflect on the lives of those interred there.

One of the most striking architectural features of the Zentralfriedhof is the Karl-Borromäus-Kirche (St. Charles Borromeo Church), a stunning Art Nouveau chapel that sits at the heart of the cemetery. Designed by the Austrian architect Max Hegele, the church was completed in 1911 and is one of the finest examples of Art Nouveau (Jugendstil) architecture in Vienna.

St. Charles Borromeo Church

Its dome and classical lines, along with the angelic sculptures adorning the exterior, give it a serene and majestic presence. The Karl-Borromäus-Kirche also plays a central role in the many funeral services held at the cemetery and is an iconic symbol of the Zentralfriedhof itself.

The cemetery is divided into numerous sections, each designated for different religious denominations, social classes, and notable figures. The most famous section is Group 32A, the Musiker section, which contains the graves of many of Vienna's greatest composers. This area is often a place of pilgrimage for classical music lovers from around the world, drawn to pay homage to figures like Ludwig van Beethoven, Franz Schubert, Johannes Brahms, and Johann Strauss II.

Zentralfriedhof is also home to various war memorials, including those for soldiers of World War I and II, as well as the graves of political figures, industrialists, artists, and scientists. The careful design of the cemetery, with its wide paths, grand tombs, and secluded corners, offers visitors a chance to wander and reflect, making the Zentralfriedhof more than just a place of mourning, but also a place of cultural and historical discovery.

Notable Figures Buried in the Zentralfriedhof

The Zentralfriedhof is the final resting place of over three million people, including many of Austria's most prominent historical and cultural figures. Among the most visited graves are those of Vienna's great composers, whose influence on music was so profound that their section of the cemetery is sometimes referred to as the "Pantheon of Music."

Among the composers buried in this cemetery are, among others: Ludwig van Beethoven, Johannes Brahms, Christoph Willibald Gluck, Antonio Salieri, Arnold Schönberg, Franz Schubert, Wolfgang Amadeus Mozart (cenotaph), Johann Strauss (Father), Johann Strauss (Son), Franz von Suppè, and Hugo Wolf.

Ludwig van Beethoven was reinterred at the Zentralfriedhof in 1888, 61 years after his death, as part of an effort to honor his legacy in Vienna. His grave is a site of pilgrimage for musicians and music lovers alike, and a statue of the composer watches over his tomb.

Franz Schubert, like Beethoven, was moved to the Zentralfriedhof after his death, and his tomb lies next to Beethoven's, symbolizing the connection between the two composers during their lives and after.

Johann Strauss II, known as the "Waltz King," is buried in the same section, his grave often adorned with flowers left by admirers of his music. Strauss's music, especially the famous "Blue Danube Waltz," is synonymous with Vienna and Austrian culture.

Johannes Brahms, one of the leading composers of the Romantic period, is also buried in this section. His grave is simple yet elegant, reflecting his serious and humble nature.

Aside from the composers, many other luminaries rest in the Zentralfriedhof:

Arthur Schnitzler

Arthur Schnitzler, the famous playwright and author, lies in the Jewish section of the cemetery. Schnitzler's works, including *La Ronde* and *Dream Story* (which was the basis for Stanley Kubrick's film *Eyes Wide Shut*), were deeply tied to Viennese life in the early 20th century.

Hans Kelsen, the legal philosopher who authored the Austrian Constitution, is buried here, marking his contributions to the development of law and governance in Austria.

Friedrich von Hayek, the Nobel Prize-winning economist and philosopher, also rests in the cemetery, a testament to Vienna's intellectual heritage.

Additionally, the cemetery contains memorials for many who lost their lives during the world wars. The Russian Orthodox section, for example, contains graves of soldiers from both world wars, while the Jewish section poignantly reminds visitors of the many lives lost during the Holocaust.

The fallen from every war fought in Austria lie here side by side.

The Zentralfriedhof in Viennese Culture

The Zentralfriedhof holds a unique place in Viennese culture, reflecting the city's longstanding relationship with death and the macabre. While it is a place of mourning and remembrance, it is also deeply intertwined with the Viennese sense of humor and philosophical outlook on life and death. The cemetery has been immortalized in songs, films, and literature, often reflecting the Viennese attitude that death is not something to be feared, but rather an inevitable part of life to be confronted with a mix of reverence, irony, and even humor.

One of the most famous songs associated with the Zentralfriedhof is **"Der Herrgott weiß, wann der Zentralfriedhof ruft"** ("The Lord Knows When the Zentralfriedhof Calls"), by the Austrian singer and actor Wolfgang Ambros. The song humorously reflects on the idea that, in the end, everyone will be called to the cemetery, no matter their station in life. This playful yet fatalistic attitude toward death is characteristic of Viennese culture, where the inevitability of death is accepted with a mixture of somber respect and sardonic wit.

The cemetery also plays a role in the annual **All Saints' Day** (Allerheiligen) and **All Souls' Day** (Allerseelen) traditions, when families visit the graves of loved ones, lighting candles and leaving flowers in a moving display of reverence and remembrance. These days of observance draw thousands of visitors to the Zentralfriedhof, transforming it into a place of light and reflection, where the dead are honored by the living.

Austrian presidents and their spouses are laid to rest in the President's Crypt (Präsidentengruft) located in front of the church.

Whether you visit to pay respects to the city's great composers, to wander the tree-lined avenues in quiet contemplation, or to reflect on the human condition, the Zentralfriedhof offers an experience that is both deeply personal and profoundly universal.

Zentralfriedhof | Central Cemetery

Address: Simmeringer Hauptstraße 234, 1110 Vienna

Public transport: U3 to Simmering; Tram 6, 71 to Zentralfriedhof

Opening hours: Daily: 7 a.m. – 6 p.m.

Online: www.friedhoefewien.at

HISTORY OF VIENNA

Long before Vienna became the bustling capital of Austria, known for its majestic palaces, musical prowess, and rich cultural tapestry, it was a land that bore witness to the ebb and flow of ancient civilizations. Diving into the story of Vienna, or Vindobona as it was known in ancient times, is akin to unearthing a hidden chapter of a book that many of us thought we knew.

This journey into Vienna's past reveals not just the city's origins but also offers a fascinating glimpse into the life and times of its earliest inhabitants. In the shadows of Vienna's modern architecture lie the remnants of Vindobona, a Roman military camp established in the first century AD. This camp was part of a network of fortifications along the Danube River, serving as a crucial defensive line against the Germanic tribes to the north.

The choice of Vienna as a strategic location underscores the importance of geography in the annals of history—a theme as relevant today as it was two millennia ago. With their unparalleled knack for military strategy and urban planning, the Romans saw the potential in the gentle curves of the Danube and the fertile lands surrounding it.

Schweizertor - The oldest part of the Hofburg

Vindobona might not have been as grand as Rome or as scholarly as Alexandria, but it was a bustling center in its own right. Its streets were filled with soldiers, merchants, and artisans. The blend of Roman architectural prowess with the lush, green landscapes of the region must have been a sight to behold. Imagine the Roman baths, forums, and temples, interspersed with the local Celtic influences, creating a cultural mosaic as vibrant as any in the sprawling Roman Empire.

The daily life in Vindobona was a testament to the ingenuity and adaptability of its inhabitants. The Romans introduced advanced urban planning techniques, including sophisticated water systems and paved roads, which were marvels of engineering at the time. These innovations not only improved the quality of life for the residents but also laid the groundwork for the city's future development. These remnants are still seen in Vienna today, a silent testament to the city's ancient roots.

However, life in ancient Vienna was not just about military might and architectural advancements. The intersection of various cultures—Roman settlers, local Celtic tribes, and, later, Germanic peoples—created a melting pot of traditions, languages, and beliefs. This fusion of cultures is reflected in the archaeological finds from the area, which include Roman artifacts adorned with Celtic motifs and Germanic weapons made with Roman techniques. It's a reminder of the complex tapestry of human history, where cultures blend and evolve, leaving behind a rich legacy for future generations.

As the Roman Empire began to wane, Vindobona, like many of its outposts, faced its share of challenges. The decline brought about by waves of invasions and internal decay eventually led to the fall of the Roman presence in the region. However, the end of the Roman era did not mean the end of Vienna's story. Instead, it marked the beginning of a new chapter, as the land that once housed a Roman camp gradually evolved into the city we know today.

Reflecting on Vienna's ancient past reminds us that the cities we live in and visit do not just point in time but are part of a continuum that stretches back centuries. The streets of Vienna, with their blend of historical and modern architecture, are a living museum, telling the story of human civilization's resilience, adaptability, and creativity.

As we walk through Vienna's historic districts, let us remember the layers of history beneath our feet. From the Celtic tribes who first settled the land to the Roman soldiers who fortified it and the countless generations that followed, each has contributed to the tapestry that makes Vienna a city like no other. In the grandeur of its palaces and the quiet beauty of its parks, the spirit of Vindobona lives on a bridge connecting the past, present, and future.

Roman Emperor Marcus Aurelius in Vindobona

The story of Marcus Aurelius in Vindobona is a captivating chapter in the rich tapestry of Vienna's ancient history. Marcus Aurelius, known as one of the last of the Five Good Emperors of the Roman Empire, was not only a stoic philosopher but also a ruler who faced the complexities and challenges of governance head-on. His presence in Vindobona, modern-day Vienna, intertwines the city's past with Rome's philosophical and military endeavors at its zenith.

Hoher Markt featuring the Anker Clock by Franz Matsch (1914)

Around the middle of the 2nd century AD, amidst the Marcomannic Wars, Marcus Aurelius found himself in the Danubian provinces, including the area around Vindobona. These wars were fought between the Roman Empire and Germanic tribes, along with other nomadic groups. Vindobona, situated strategically along the Danube River, was a critical military base from which Marcus Aurelius could oversee and command his legions.

The city's location was pivotal. It acted as a bulwark against incursions from the north and played a significant role in the empire's defensive network.

Marcus Aurelius, often depicted as a philosopher-king, brought to Vindobona the might of Roman arms and the depth of stoic thought. It's intriguing to imagine him, amid military campaigns, reflecting on the nature of duty, virtue, and the impermanence of life—themes central to his philosophical meditations. His time in Vindobona underscores a period where leadership challenges, the hardships of war, and the pursuit of wisdom converged.

The emperor's presence in the region was not merely about war; it was also a significant chapter in the Romanization of the area. Under his reign and through establishing military camps like Vindobona, Roman culture, language, and technology permeated the local societies. These interactions laid the groundwork for the multicultural tapestry that characterized the later history of Vienna and its surroundings.

The legacy of Marcus Aurelius in Vindobona, and indeed across the Roman Empire, is multifaceted. On one hand, his military campaigns contributed to the security and expansion of Rome's borders. On the other, his philosophical writings, especially "Meditations," composed during his campaigns, have left an indelible mark on Western thought. The juxtaposition of a Roman emperor, stoic philosopher, and military commander spending time in what is now Vienna adds a layer of historical and intellectual depth to the city's past.

Today, while walking through Vienna, one might need help to observe traces of Marcus Aurelius's presence directly. Yet, the legacy of Roman occupation and the strategic importance of Vindobona in antiquity is palpable. Museums in Vienna house artifacts from this era, and archaeological sites offer glimpses into the city's Roman past. Furthermore, Marcus Aurelius's philosophical legacy, emphasizing reason, duty, and the common good, resonates beyond history's confines, contributing to Vienna's cultural and intellectual heritage.

Movie Gladiator and Vindobona

In Ridley Scott's cinematic masterpiece Gladiator, the grandeur and turmoil of the Roman Empire are brought vividly to life through the eyes of Maximus Decimus Meridius, a Roman general turned gladiator. While the film takes liberties with historical accuracy for the sake of drama, it touches upon the figure of Emperor Marcus Aurelius, a stoic philosopher-king whose reign is remembered as wisdom and justice. Marcus Aurelius spent considerable time in military campaigns along the Danube frontier, including Vindobona, present-day Vienna.

Although "Gladiator" is a work of fiction, its backdrop of Roman military might and Marcus Aurelius's philosophical demeanor invite viewers to explore the historical realities of places like Vindobona. The movie, in its essence, reminds viewers of the rich tapestry of history that cities like Vienna are built upon and the enduring legacy of figures like Marcus Aurelius, whose philosophies continue to resonate long after their time.

Vienna in the Middle Ages

Nestled along the banks of the Danube, the medieval city of Vienna presents a fascinating chapter in the annals of European history. As we peel back the layers of time, Vienna during the Middle Ages emerged as a geographical location and a vibrant stage where the dramas of politics, culture, and society played out. This period, stretching roughly from the fall of the Roman Empire to the dawn of the Renaissance, saw Vienna transform from a modest settlement into a bustling medieval city, a beacon of power and culture in the heart of Europe.

The early Middle Ages marked a time of transition for Vienna. With the decline of Roman influence, the region saw a flux of peoples and cultures, each leaving its mark on the burgeoning city.

St. Stephen's Cathedral

The Bavarians, Slavs, and later the Magyars all shaped the early medieval landscape of Vienna. It was a time of constant change, with the city's identity and boundaries continually evolving. Yet, through these shifts, Vienna began to emerge as a strategic crossroads, its importance underscored by its location at the nexus of trade routes that connected the continent's north and south, east and west.

The turning point in Vienna's medieval history came with the Babenberg dynasty, which took control in the 10th century. Under the Babenbergs, Vienna flourished as a center of trade and commerce.

The establishment of the Ostarrîchi (Austria) in 996 AD, with Vienna at its heart, was a moment of profound significance, marking the city's growing prominence on the European stage. The construction of St. Stephen's Cathedral in the 12th century, a marvel of Gothic architecture that still dominates Vienna's skyline, symbolized the city's burgeoning wealth and influence.

However, the Middle Ages were not just a time of growth and prosperity but also marked by hardship and conflict. The city saw its share of sieges and battles, most notably during the Crusades and in conflicts with neighboring realms. The siege of Vienna by the Mongols in 1241 is a testament to the city's strategic importance and resilience. Despite these challenges, Vienna continued to grow, its walls expanding to accommodate the increasing population and its markets bustling with goods worldwide.

The Vergilius Chapel, or Virgilkapelle, is an underground crypt (early 13th century) in the Underground Station U1, U3 Stephansplatz

The late Middle Ages saw Vienna further cement its cultural and political hub status. The University of Vienna, founded in 1365, became a center of learning and scholarship, attracting students and intellectuals from across Europe. The city's governance also evolved, establishing the Vienna City Council in 1221, which laid the foundations for civic administration and law.

The transition of power from the Babenberg to the Habsburg dynasty in the late Middle Ages marked the beginning of a new era for Vienna. The Habsburgs, who would come to dominate European politics for centuries, made Vienna their imperial seat, transforming it into a city of immense political and cultural significance. Under their rule, Vienna began to take on the grandeur and sophistication that would define it in the Renaissance and beyond.

Reflecting on Vienna's medieval past, we are reminded of the city's enduring ability to adapt and thrive amid the vicissitudes of history. From a strategic outpost on the Danube to a flourishing medieval city, Vienna's journey through the Middle Ages is a testament to its people's resilience, creativity, and spirit. The architectural marvels, the scholarly pursuits, and the bustling markets of medieval Vienna laid the groundwork for the city's future as a beacon of culture, learning, and power in Europe.

Today, as we wander through the cobblestone streets of Vienna, past the shadows of its Gothic cathedrals and into the quiet courtyards of its ancient universities, we are walking through layers of history, each step a reminder of the city's rich and tumultuous past. With all their complexity and contradiction, the Middle Ages remain alive in the fabric of modern Vienna, a bridge connecting the present with the deep and enduring legacy of the past.

Vienna Under the Habsburg Dynasty

The Habsburg dynasty, one of the most influential royal houses in European history, left an indelible mark on Vienna, shaping the city's destiny for over six centuries. From the late Middle Ages to the collapse of the Austro-Hungarian Empire at the end of World War I, the Habsburgs transformed Vienna into a vibrant epicenter of political power, cultural innovation, and architectural grandeur.

Streets of Vienna

The Rise of Vienna as a Habsburg Powerhouse

The story of Vienna under the Habsburgs is, in many ways, a city coming into its own. When the Habsburgs ascended to power in the late 13th century, Vienna was already recognized for its strategic importance, nestled along vital European trade routes. However, it was under the Habsburgs, especially from the reign of Maximilian I onwards, that Vienna began transforming into a truly imperial city.

The Habsburgs were masterful in leveraging Vienna's geographical and political position to enhance their power, using the city as a base to administer their vast and diverse empire. The construction of the Hofburg Palace, which began in earnest under Emperor Maximilian II, symbolized Vienna's status as the heart of the Habsburg realm. Over the centuries, this sprawling complex grew to reflect the Habsburg rulers' wealth, power, and artistic tastes, serving as a residence, governmental center, and cultural hub.

A Cultural and Intellectual Beacon

Perhaps more than any other aspect, the Habsburg dynasty is renowned for its patronage of the arts and sciences, a legacy deeply imprinted on Vienna's cultural landscape.

The dynasty's support for composers like Mozart, Beethoven, and Haydn turned Vienna into the world's music capital, a title the city still proudly holds today. Opera, theater, and the visual arts flourished, with magnificent baroque and rococo buildings like Schönbrunn Palace and Belvedere Palace serving as residences and cultural venues.

The founding of the University of Vienna in 1365 laid the groundwork for the city's reputation as a center of learning and scholarship. Under the Habsburgs, the university expanded its faculties and influence, attracting students and intellectuals from across Europe. The Austrian National Library, with its grandiose State Hall, is another testament to the Habsburgs' commitment to knowledge. It houses millions of volumes, including rare manuscripts and incunabula.

The Sieges of Vienna

The city of Vienna experienced two significant sieges by the Ottoman Empire, events that profoundly impacted European history and shaped the continent's political landscape. These sieges, occurring in 1529 and 1683, represented pivotal moments in the longstanding conflict between the Habsburgs and the Ottomans, and they epitomized the clash between Christian Europe and the Muslim East.

The First Siege of Vienna (1529)

The first siege of Vienna in 1529 marked the Ottoman Empire's initial major attempt to establish its hegemony in Central Europe. Led by Sultan Suleiman the Magnificent, the Ottoman forces advanced with a large army, aiming to capture Vienna and use it as a base for further expansion into Europe. The city at that time was not the massive fortress it would later become; its defenses were relatively modest, making it vulnerable to such a formidable force.

Equestrian statue at the Palais Montenuovo - Ottoman attackers managed to dig a tunnel under the city walls all the way to that spot (1529)

Despite these vulnerabilities, the siege failed due to a combination of factors. Under the leadership of Niklas Graf Salm and Wilhelm von Roggendorf, the defenders effectively utilized the city's fortifications. Moreover, the onset of cold weather, logistical challenges, and heavy rains hindered the Ottoman army's ability to maintain a prolonged siege. As a result, Suleiman was forced to retreat, marking the siege as a failure but also a significant warning to the rest of Europe about the Ottoman threat.

The Second Siege of Vienna (1683)

The second siege, occurring more than a century and a half later, in 1683, was a much more dramatic and decisive encounter. This time, the Ottomans were led by Grand Vizier Kara Mustafa Pasha, who laid siege to Vienna with an even larger force. Vienna, now significantly better fortified and prepared, was under the command of Ernst Rüdiger Graf von Starhemberg, who was determined to hold the city against the Ottoman onslaught.

Kahlenberg - Site of the decisive battle for Vienna (1683)

The 1683 siege reached a critical point when, after weeks of siege, the city was on the verge of capitulation. However, a relieving force consisting of Polish, Austrian, and German troops led by King John III Sobieski of Poland arrived in the nick of time.

Sobieski's cavalry, famously known as the "Winged Hussars," played a crucial role in a decisive battle on the Kahlenberg Mountain outside Vienna. The battle ended in a catastrophic defeat for the Ottoman forces, marking the beginning of the decline of Ottoman influence in Europe.

Social and Urban Transformation

The Habsburg era also saw significant social and urban development in Vienna. The dynasty's centralizing policies and the administrative needs of a growing empire necessitated a well-organized urban plan. The expansion of the city's boundaries, the construction of the Ringstraße with its public buildings, parks, and monuments in the 19th century, and the development of a modern infrastructure reflected Vienna's status as a global metropolis.

Moreover, the Habsburgs' complex marriage policies and political alliances brought an influx of different nationalities into Vienna, making it a melting pot of cultures, languages, and traditions. This multicultural environment contributed to the city's dynamic social fabric, influencing its cuisine, festivals, and everyday life.

The Pharmacy of the White Angel by Oskar Laske, Bognergasse 9

The fall of the Austro-Hungarian Empire in 1918 marked the end of the Habsburg dynasty's direct rule over Vienna, but their reign left an unmistakable legacy.

The architectural splendors, the cultural institutions, and the spirit of Vienna bear the imprint of the Habsburgs' ambitious vision.

Under the Habsburgs, Vienna was not just a city of kings and emperors but a canvas upon which the story of a continent was painted in bold and vibrant strokes.

Wien Museum

Nestled in the heart of Vienna, the Wien Museum is a central point to the city's rich cultural history, from its ancient origins to its present-day status as a vibrant, modern metropolis.

The Wien Museum's collections are as diverse as the city's history. They include fine arts, architectural models, archaeological finds, and ephemera related to Vienna's urban development. The museum holds several centuries-old artworks, including masterpieces by Gustav Klimt, Egon Schiele, and Richard Gerstl.

Its historical artifacts provide insights into everyday life in Vienna through the ages, from medieval times to the dynamic era of the Habsburg monarchy and into the 20th century. One of the museum's major strengths is its comprehensive collection of architectural models and plans, which document the transformation of Vienna's urban landscape. These include detailed models of historic buildings and districts, providing a visual narrative of the city's architectural evolution.

Wien Museum Karlsplatz | Vienna Museum

Address: Karlsplatz 8, 1040 Vienna

Online: www.wienmuseum.at

Public transport: Underground: U1, U2, U4 Karlsplatz

Hours: Tue-Fri 9 a.m. – 6 p.m., Sat-Sun 10 a.m. – 6 p.m.

Roman Museum Vienna

The Römermuseum Wien, or the Roman Museum Vienna, is a fascinating portal into the rich Roman history in Vienna, Austria. Located in the city's heart, this museum is a repository of artifacts and a narrative hub connecting the past with the present, offering insights into the region's Roman military, social, and architectural influence.

Vienna, known in ancient times as Vindobona, was a significant Roman military camp that formed part of the Limes Romanus, the frontier of the Roman Empire.

Established in the first century AD, Vindobona served as a strategic site for the Roman legions, particularly in their endeavors to secure the empire's borders against Germanic tribes.

The discovery of these ancient ruins in modern Vienna led to the establishment of the Römermuseum, which is situated directly above the remains of the Roman officer's quarters.

The Römermuseum Wien boasts an impressive collection of Roman artifacts, including tools, coins, military equipment, and personal items that vividly depict daily life in a Roman garrison.

One of the museum's standout features is its detailed reconstruction of Roman buildings, including a partially reconstructed Roman house complete with furnishings and decor. These reconstructions are based on extensive archaeological research and provide a tangible connection to the past.

Römermuseum Wien | Roman Museum Vienna

Address: Hoher Markt 3, 1010 Vienna

Online: www.wienmuseum.at/roemermuseum

Public transport: Public transport: Underground: U1, U3 Stephansplatz

Hours: Tue-Fri 9 a.m. – 6 p.m., Sat-Sun 10 a.m. – 6 p.m.

TIMELINE OF VIENNA

This timeline outlines the key events that have significantly influenced the development of Vienna.

1st-millennium BC – Vindobona settled.

180 – Roman emperor Marcus Aurelius dies in Vindobona.

740 – The Church of St Ruprecht, the oldest church in Vienna, was first built.

881 – The Bavarians had their first clash at Wenia with the Hungarians. It was the first mention of Vienna.

1030 – The Hungarians besiege Vienna.

1155 – Henry II, Duke of Austria, appoints Vienna as a capital city.

1160 – St. Stephen's Cathedral built.

1221 – Vienna receives rights as the staple port.

1237 – Vienna received a freedom charter from Frederick II., confirmed in 1247.

1276 – King Ottokar II of Bohemia laid the foundation stone for the Minorites Church.

1278 – City charter granted.

1280 – Jans der Enikel writes the Fürstenbuch, the first history of the city.

1349 – Augustinian Church consecrated.

1365 – The University of Vienna was founded.

1421 – Jews expelled.

1482 – Johann Winterburger sets up the printing press.

1485 – Siege of Vienna by the Kingdom of Hungary, the city passed to Hungary. Royal Court of King Matthias Corvinus of Hungary relocated to Vienna, known as Bécs in Hungarian.

1529 – Siege of Vienna by the Ottoman Army. Vienna successfully withstood a siege lasting just over two weeks, from September 27 to October 15, 1529.

1556 – Vienna becomes the seat of the Holy Roman Empire under Ferdinand I.

1598 – Donaukanal regulated.

1643 – Schönbrunn Palace built.

1679 – Great Plague of Vienna.

1683 – Siege of Vienna (July 17–September 12, 1683): This military campaign involved the Ottomans advancing against the Habsburg Holy Roman Emperor Leopold I. The siege ended in defeat for the Ottomans at the hands of a coalition force under the leadership of John III Sobieski of Poland. The successful defense marked a turning point, signaling the decline of Ottoman influence in Eastern Europe.

1684 – Kollschitzky coffeehouse in business.

1692 – Academy of Fine Arts Vienna founded.

1702 – Palais Strozzi completed.

1703 – Palais Liechtenstein built.

1704 – Linienwall fortification built.

1709 – Theater am Kärntnertor built.

1713 – Plague epidemic.

1716 – Palais Kinsky completed.

1718 – Vienna Porcelain Manufactory was founded.

1724 – Population 150,000.

1735 – Winter Riding School built.

1741 – Burgtheater opens.

1762 – Premiere of Gluck's opera Orfeo ed Euridice.

1765 – Tiergarten Schönbrunn (zoo) opens.

1766 – Prater opens.

1772 – Freyung Christmas market begins.

1781 – Mozart arrives in Vienna from Salzburg.

1786 – Premiere of Mozart's Marriage of Figaro.

1786 – Demel Confectionery and Gesellschaft der Associierten founded.

1790 – Population: 200,000.

1791 – 30 September: Premiere of Mozart's The Magic Flute.

1791 – Wolfgang Amadeus Mozart dies.

1792 – Schweighofer piano manufactury established.

1792 – Beethoven arrives in Vienna from Bonn.

1797 – 31 January: Franz Peter Schubert is born in Alsergrund, Wien.

1800 – 2 April: Premiere of Beethoven's Symphony No. 1.

1805 – 23 May: Premiere of Beethoven's opera Fidelio.

1805 – 13 November: Napoleon takes the city.

1808 – 22 December: premiere of Beethoven's Fifth and Sixth Symphonies, Choral Fantasy, and Piano Concerto No. 4 at the Theater an der Wien.

1809 – Battle of Aspern-Essling. Napoleon crossed the Danube near Vienna, but the French and their allies were attacked and forced back across the river by the Austrians under Archduke Charles.

1809 – Joseph Haydn dies.

1814 – The Congress of Vienna, about Europe after Napoleon.

1824 – 7 May: premiere of Beethoven's Symphony No. 9.

1827 – 27 March: Ludwig van Beethoven dies.

1828 – 19 November: Franz Peter Schubert dies.

1832 – Sachertorte invented.

1840 – Population 231,050.

1847 – The Austrian Academy of Sciences was established.

1848 – Vienna Uprising: On March 13, a revolution erupted in Vienna, resulting in the ousting of State Chancellor Metternich, the establishment of press freedom, and the declaration of a constitution. The most significant legislation enacted during this period was the law abolishing all feudal obligations imposed on peasants.

1850 – The City expanded beyond Innere Stadt (1st district).

1850 – Population 551,300.

1858 – Ringstraße constructed.

1860-1864 – The tower of the Cathedral of St Stephen was re-built.

1864 – Neue Freie Presse newspaper begins publication.

1869 – Vienna State Opera house built.

1869 – Population 842,951.

1870 – Danube regulation

1870 – Musikverein inaugurated.

1873 – World exposition in Vienna.

1873 – Café Landtmann and Hotel Imperial in business.

1874 – Premiere of Strauss's opera Die Fledermaus.

1875 – Danube levees constructed.

1876 – Academy of Fine Arts building erected.

1876 – Hotel Sacher established.

1876 – Café Central in business.

1880 – Café Sperl in business.

1880 – Population 1,090,119.

1881 – Palace of Justice built.

1882 – Palmenhaus Schönbrunn opens.

1883 – Completion of the Vienna City Hall.

1886 – Hermesvilla built. Emperor Franz Joseph I gave it to his wife, Empress Elisabeth.

1887 – The Historical Museum of Vienna was established.

1889 – Rudolf, Crown Prince of Austria, the only son of the Imperial couple, was buried in the Imperial Crypt. The cause of death was suicide.

1890 – Population 1,364,548.

1891 – Kunsthistorisches Museum opens.

1897 – Wiener Riesenrad erected.

1897 – Vienna Secession art group founded.

1898 – The Empress of Austria was buried in the Imperial Crypt. The Empress was assassinated in Geneva, Switzerland.

1898 – Wiener Stadtbahn begins to work (today subways U4 and U6). The architect Otto Wagner was hired as the artistic director for the Vienna Stadtbahn project.

1898 – Secession Building constructed.

1899 – Freud's The Interpretation of Dreams published.

1900 – Population 1,769,137.

1903 – Wiener Werkstätte art group founded.

1908 – Vienna Psychoanalytic Society active.

1910 – Population 2,031,000.

1912 – Aspern Airfield opens.

1913 – 23 February: premiere of Schoenberg's Gurre-Lieder.

1914 – The assassination of Archduke Franz Ferdinand was a pivotal event that precipitated World War I. On June 28, 1914, Archduke Franz Ferdinand of Austria, the heir presumptive to the Austro-Hungarian throne, and his wife, Sophie, Duchess of Hohenberg, were killed in Sarajevo by Gavrilo Princip, a Bosnian Serb student. Emperor Franz Joseph interpreted this act as an affront to the dynasty's honor and consequently declared war on Serbia, which he believed was behind the assassination. This war extended from July 28, 1914, to November 11, 1918.

1916 – 30 November: funeral of Franz Joseph I of Austria.

1920 – The Austrian National Library was established.

1938 – Anschluss. In March 1938, Germany annexed neighboring Austria.

1942 – The Allies begin the bombing of Vienna.

1943 – 30 August: Vienna-Schwechat subcamp of the Mauthausen concentration camp was established. Its prisoners were mostly Polish, Soviet, Italian and Spanish.

1945 – Battle for Vienna. City under Allied occupation.

1954 – Vienna International Airport opens.

1954 – Flood in Vienna.

1955 – On May 15, 1955, delegates from the Soviet Union, Great Britain, the United States, and France inked an accord bestowing independence upon Austria and coordinating the departure of all occupying military units.

1957 – International Atomic Energy Agency headquartered in Vienna.

1961 – Vienna summit of USA and USSR.

1969 – OPEC headquarters moves from Geneva, Switzerland to Vienna.

1976 – Vienna U-Bahn (subway) opens.

1979 – UNO City built. The United Nations Office in Vienna is one of the four major office sites of the United Nations, hosting a collective presence of various UN agencies.

1988 – New Danube channel constructed.

1989 – Zita of Bourbon-Parma, the last crowned empress of the Habsburg Monarchy, is buried in the Imperial Crypt.

1992 – The biggest AIDS charity event in Europe, the Life Ball, begins.

1993 – World Conference on Human Rights held.

1995 – The Secretariat for the Organization for Security and Co-operation in Europe was established.

2007 – EU Fundamental Rights Agency established.

2008 – The IAEA Secretariat was headquartered at the Vienna International Centre.

2008 – UEFA European Football Championship held.

2011 – Otto von Habsburg's funeral. He is buried in the Imperial Crypt. He was the last crown prince of Austria-Hungary.

2014– Population 1,797,337.

2009 – 2019: For ten years, the international consulting firm Mercer conducted an annual global study evaluating the quality of life in major cities worldwide. Vienna consistently held the top position throughout this period.

2023 – Vienna secured first place in quality of life rankings conducted by The Economist and Monocle.

2024 – Population 2,002,821.

TELL US ABOUT YOUR EXPERIENCE

Thank You for Reading!

Reaching the final page of this journey means the world to me. I'd be incredibly grateful if you could take just 60 seconds to leave a review on Amazon.

How to Leave a Review:

Scan the QR Code: Open your phone's camera and follow the link.

Or Visit:

www.amazon.com/review/create-review/?asin=3991820048

If you ordered from a different Amazon store (e.g., amazon.co.uk, amazon.ca), just replace **.com** with the appropriate domain.

Thank you again for your time. It's readers like you who make this work so fulfilling.

Warm regards,

Maximilian Just,

author

Printed in Great Britain
by Amazon

59549517R00086